"*Glory in the Ordinary* is a ne[...] of work within the home. Cour[...] small ways builds a lifetime of glorifying God. The simple tasks of cooking a meal, taking out the trash, fixing a car, or washing laundry might seem mundane, but offered to God, these daily tasks have kingdom significance."

 Melissa Kruger, Women's Ministry Coordinator, Uptown Church, Charlotte, North Carolina; author, *The Envy of Eve*; Editor, The Gospel Coalition; blogger, *Wit's End*

"Have you ever considered the significance of your work at home? Everyone needs encouragement in his or her work, and in *Glory in the Ordinary*, Courtney Reissig provides just that. Reissig shares honestly and humbly about the various temptations and struggles of at-home work, reminding us that our work—from cleaning dishes to wiping runny noses—is good and meaningful work, ultimately because it's meaningful to God."

 Trillia Newbell, author, *Enjoy*, *Fear and Faith*, and *United*

"Living in daily life what an author writes in a book is the sure mark of authenticity, and Courtney passes that test well. She invites God into every area of her life, especially her home. I love seeing young women choose the often lonely and thankless road of mommy-land knowing the rewards will come one day, if not from grownup children, from a Father who sees all and is pleased with her sacrifice and service in his name."

 Barbara Rainey, Cofounder, FamilyLife; author, *Letters to My Daughters: The Art of Being a Wife*

"From the invigorating depths of theological reflection as well as personal life experience as a stay-at-home mom, Courtney Reissig opens our minds and captures our hearts to the messy grandeur of noncompensatory work. *Glory in the Ordinary* adeptly maintains gospel-centricity and cultural relevance while making a persuasive case that neighborly love begins in the place we call home. Whether you are presently a stay-at-home mom or your workplace is outside the home, *Glory in the Ordinary* will help you better connect Sunday to Monday with a more integral, coherent, and seamless gospel faith. This is a book that needed to be written, one I have been waiting for. I highly recommend it."

 Tom Nelson, author, *Work Matters*; Senior Pastor, Christ Community Church, Overland Park, Kansas; President, Made to Flourish

"*Ordinary* is a word that perfectly describes my life and the lives of most women in my church and community. Each day presents a fresh to-do list that looks remarkably like the one from yesterday—and the one from last year: lunches and laundry, dishes and dusting, gardening and grocery shopping. But with warmth and wisdom Courtney Reissig opens our eyes to God's glory in this ordinary. Exploring questions of identity, community, service, and rest, Reissig sets work in the home in its historic and biblical context and gives meaning to our mundane. Whether your priorities include gleaming windows or PB&J for six, this book will help you to value your work in the home because God himself values it. That dirty floor can wait. Read and be encouraged."

Megan Hill, writer; speaker; pastor's wife; author, *Praying Together*; contributor, The Gospel Coalition and *CT* Women; editorial board member, *Christianity Today* Magazine

"As one who never expected to work in the home, this book is refreshing, gospel-saturated encouragement for all of us who are knee-deep in laundry, childcare, and dishes. Be prepared to see your work in a whole new way: with joy, for the kingdom, and with eternity in view."

Christina Fox, writer; speaker; author, *A Heart Set Free: A Journey to Hope through the Psalms of Lament*

"I'm thankful Courtney has joined the generations of wise women who build their homes (Prov. 14:1). Her book affirms the dignity and worth of homemaking and homekeeping, even as it reminds us that such work is faithfully loving our closest neighbors: the ones who live under our own roofs."

Candice Watters, Cofounder, Boundless.org; author, *Get Married: What Women Can Do to Help It Happen*

Glory in the Ordinary

Glory in the Ordinary

*Why Your Work in the Home
Matters to God*

COURTNEY REISSIG

WHEATON, ILLINOIS

Glory in the Ordinary: Why Your Work in the Home Matters to God

Copyright © 2017 by Courtney Reissig

Published by Crossway
   1300 Crescent Street
   Wheaton, Illinois 60187

Published in association with the literary agency of Wolgemuth & Associates, Inc.

Cover design: Crystal Courtney

First printing 2017

Printed in the United States of America

Scripture quotations are from the ESV® Bible (The Holy Bible, English Standard Version®), copyright © 2001 by Crossway, a publishing ministry of Good News Publishers. Used by permission. All rights reserved.

Trade paperback ISBN: 978-1-4335-5267-0
ePub ISBN: 978-1-4335-5270-0
PDF ISBN: 978-1-4335-5268-7
Mobipocket ISBN: 978-1-4335-5269-4

Library of Congress Cataloging-in-Publication Data

Names: Reissig, Courtney, 1983– author.
Title: Glory in the ordinary : why your work in the home matters to God / Courtney Reissig.
Description: Wheaton : Crossway, 2017. | Includes bibliographical references and index.
Identifiers: LCCN 2016041199 (print) | LCCN 2017006409 (ebook) | ISBN 9781433552670 (tp) | ISBN 9781433552687 (pdf) | ISBN 9781433552694 (mobi) | ISBN 9781433552700 (epub)
Subjects: LCSH: Wives—Religious life. | Homemakers—Religious life. | Christian women—Religious life. | Home economics. | Home—Religious aspects—Christianity.
Classification: LCC BV4528.15 .R45 2017 (print) | LCC BV4528.15 (ebook) | DDC 248.8/435—dc23
LC record available at https://lccn.loc.gov/2016041199

Crossway is a publishing ministry of Good News Publishers.

BP		27	26	25	24	23	22	21	20	19	18	17
15	14	13	12	11	10	9	8	7	6	5	4	3	2	1

To my parents, Rick and Deb Tarter
For showing me the value and dignity of
ordinary work, knowing that in the Lord my
work is never in vain (1 Cor. 15:58).

Contents

Acknowledgments

No one's work is done in isolation, even the work of writing a book. Of course, my name might be on the cover, but I am not the only one responsible for this book. It took a whole community of people to get this book finished.

It's a joy to work with such great people as the team at Crossway. Thank you especially to Tara Davis, Dave DeWit, Amy Kruis, and Lauren Harvey for believing in this book, working to make it better, and spreading its message. I consider it a privilege to partner with you.

My agent, Erik Wolgemuth, has been a great friend and encourager throughout the entire publishing process. It's a joy to work with you.

Thank you to the Gospel Coalition for first giving me a category for thinking biblically about my work, but for also giving me a platform to process this journey in the form of this book. I'm honored to work alongside such a godly team of people.

You will read a variety of stories of women in this book. These are real women who took time to talk to me about their work in the home. Thank you to Carla Jaynes, Tovey Schmidt, Julia Straub, Leanne Jenkins, Sara Bledsoe, Laura Breeding, Rachael Newton, Emily Tarter, Rachael Metcalf, Kaileigh Mobbs,

Miriam Poteet, Cecile Bledsoe, Callie Cate, Carol Jenkins, Hannah Anderson, Trillia Newbell, Jen Wilkin, Megan Hill, and Gloria Furman.

Thank you to my dear friend, Robin Ricks, for gladly watching my kids so I could leave the house to write, and for doing my laundry when you saw it piling up. You are a gift to me and to the church.

I'm greatly indebted to the people who took time to read parts (or all) of the manuscript and provide feedback. Anything good you read is owing to their help—many words were cut (which was painful but good!) and many thoughts were clarified because of them. My brother and sister-in-law, Zach and Emily Tarter, have proven so helpful for their dialogue, feedback, and care for the topic and my own engagement of it. Megan Hill carefully read a number of chapters, helped me clarify my thoughts, and brought her keen editorial eye as a former English teacher. Thanks for reading my book when you had your own book to work on, friend. Laura Breeding read every chapter of this book, and brought her helpful perspective with honesty and wisdom. Miriam Poteet was a source of encouragement both in our frequent conversations about the book and her thoughts on draft chapters.

None of this would have even happened if it weren't for Bethany Jenkins nudging me to think about writing a book on this topic. She saw something before I did, pointed me in the direction of resources that would stretch me and grow me, and cheered me on along the way. You are a good friend and a faithful editor.

My husband, Daniel, again has proven to be a source of strength and rest for me. It sounds cliché, but none of this would be possible if it weren't for his support and belief that I have something to contribute to this conversation. Thank you for believing in my voice, for being honest with me, and for loving me throughout every season—even the crazy book-writing one.

And to my kids: Luke, Zach, and Seth. I pray you will grow up to see the work God has called you to as good and valuable. It's a joy to be your momma—and it's in these ordinary days that I feel that joy most deeply.

1

The Changing Nature
of At-Home Work

Last year, I had the rare opportunity to travel without kids. I was attending a conference and, for the first time, leaving my children for longer than twenty-four hours. Because I was traveling alone, I looked like just about every other passenger on the plane. I had a book. I was dressed in clothes that I wore only if I could ensure sticky toddler fingers wouldn't stain them. And I was relaxed.

"So, what do you do for a living?" the woman sitting next to me asked. Not an uncommon airplane question—I could tell the woman was interested in small talk. I like small talk, except this time fear bubbled up inside me as I pondered how to answer. She was clearly a professional woman. I knew that because I used to be one of those women, before I had my twin boys and decided to stay home with them. Suddenly, my pride in my at-home work dwindled, and I struggled to find an answer to her question.

It's a simple question, Courtney. Just answer her honestly. You are a stay-at-home mom.

Or maybe I should tell her I'm a writer, I thought. That wouldn't have been a lie, since I had just sent in the manuscript for my first book. I am a writer. But I'm also a mom.

Since I was teetering on the edge of crying from having just left my sons for my first long trip away, it seemed fitting to go with the obvious.

"I'm a stay-at-home mom," I said nervously.

Of course, I love my kids and I love my work as a mom. I just know how it can be perceived when I actually put my vocation out there for public judgment. Not wanting to feel like a failure as a woman, I often struggle with how to respond to such a question in less conservative circles. I know that being a stay-at-home mom can be confusing to some people at best, and perceived as a waste at worst. True to my expectations, she wondered at my choice to stay home.

"I don't know how you do that all day long. I would get so bored," she said emphatically.

Should I tell her that I actually do get bored sometimes? I asked myself. But rather than starting a dialogue on how repetitive and tedious it can be to wash dishes, wipe noses, and train children, only to do it all over again the next day, I simply smiled and nodded.

True Confessions

I have a confession. I never wanted to be a stay-at-home mom—at least not when I was younger. When I hear women say that's all they ever wanted to do, I marvel. The truth is, I didn't really understand what a stay-at-home mom did. My mom stayed home with us, and I have fond memories of our time with her. She was there whenever I needed her, but to be honest, I never paid much attention to what she actually did for my brothers, my dad, and me. I viewed her work from a selfish perspective—she existed for me. And I wanted a little more for my life than servitude. While I have always loved children, I've disdained cleaning bathrooms. I've always been the one to volunteer to hold the baby, but have never been able to muster the love of baking and cooking that I assumed characterized a stay-at-home mom. What I've always loved is writing. *That* I could see myself doing.

I'm not unlike many women today who have found themselves as stay-at-home moms after not giving it much thought in their younger years. I grew up in a time when girls could be anything they wanted to be. Women now have choices and options never afforded to them before. Women can work from home while staying at home with their children. They can work outside the home while their children receive quality care from someone else. Women can stay home while still retaining their dreams and aspirations through part-time work at nap time, like I do as a writer. Women can stay home and still be praised for their choice.

So I dreamed big. A lot of other women did, too. But even with all of our high aspirations, many of us are still "opting out" of promising careers when children come along—even if we never saw ourselves doing so prior to bringing home our babies.

Journalist Louise Story tracked the career aspirations of women at elite colleges over the course of forty years.[1] Through in-depth interviews and questionnaires with current female students and faculty, and through surveying alumni, she found that many modern women, unlike their predecessors, actually aspire to stay home. More than that, even women who said forty years ago that they didn't want to stay at home, in fact, did for a period of time. In her initial article in *The New York Times*, Story noted that among graduates of Yale University and Harvard Business School, the number of women who were still working full time later in life was only around half—compared to 90 percent of their male classmates.[2] Other research confirms her findings.[3] On average, 43 percent of women will likely exit their careers for a time.[4] The reality that women end up working in the home may not have changed, but the aspirations have shifted drastically. One generation's liberation can be another generation's bondage.

But doing stay-at-home work means something completely different for me than it did for my mother and my grandmother. And in a lot of ways, that's owing to the shift in how we view the nature of at-home work itself.

From Production to Consumption

Prior to the Industrial Revolution, everyone did at-home work— even children. Because much of society was agrarian, the father often worked in the fields or cared for the livestock, while the mother often created, cleaned, and cooked. Bread needed baking, chickens needed plucking, and laundry needed mending. *All* work—for men and women—was at-home work, and it was hard work too. (This is still the reality, of course, for many men and women living in agrarian areas throughout the world.)

The Industrial Revolution, though, shifted productivity from the home to the marketplace and factories. As filmmaker Carolyn McCulley and entrepreneur Nora Shank write in *The Measure of Success*, this shift brought about "separate spheres" for men and women—men in manufacturing and business and

18

women in the home embracing the domestic life. This became known as the Golden Age of Domesticity.[5]

By the 1950s and 1960s, a single-income family with a housewife was a status symbol, and much of the laborious at-home work—by hand and from scratch—became optional for those who could afford it. With the creation of the vacuum cleaner, washer and dryer, and other modern appliances, the time it took to do traditional housework was suddenly cut in half. Bread could be bought. Clothes could be washed and dried in half the time. The home became primarily a place of consumption, not productivity.[6] For women of my grandmother's generation, the home was a place of entertainment and enjoyment of the shiny new things the post–World War II economy could buy. The housewife who used the newest cleaning products, appliances, and cooking gadgets was an aspiration to be envied. The work of the home was suddenly simplified in ways never seen before. It simply didn't take as long to cook, clean, and care for the daily tasks of the home. With children at school during the day, women had a lot of extra time on their hands. Add to this the increasingly professionalized nature of the home in the form of TV dinners, housekeepers, and even cooking shows with professional cooks, and women began to feel their amateur status and long for something different.

That extra time meant more opportunities for leisure, consumerism, and—for many—boredom. In *The Feminine Mystique*, Betty Freidan talks about a woman who wonders what to do with her newfound free time but has no options to move out of her domestic sphere. She sees her as trapped in her own home. What the Golden Age of Domesticity tried to answer about at-home work by making it a status symbol, Freidan tried to fix by making it irrelevant and beneath women. She saw the modernization of at-home work as an opportunity for women to put such menial tasks behind them. Friedan encouraged women to find their identity outside their husbands, children, and home.[7]

The Mommy Wars

By the 1980s, Friedan's clarion call to freedom launched an unexpected war between women. Since staying at home was now optional, women—especially mothers—felt the need to explain their personal decisions.

The mom who chose to stay at home felt compelled to justify her work as the best (and most sacrificial). Her orientation shifted from her husband ("housewife") to her children ("stay-at-home mom"). She was now expected to be a "full-time-playmate-for-little-kids," a provider of endless hours of entertainment.[8] She justified her work as the best choice for the kids.

The mom who chose to work outside the home felt compelled to justify her work as worthy, meaningful, and important enough to leave her children. She felt that this is what her mother fought for—her own career advancement. She focused on her talents and how to impact society, not just her 2.5 children. She quoted studies showing that working moms spend just as much time with their kids as their own mothers spent with them.[9]

Welcome to the "mommy wars." The term was created in the late 1980s by *Child Magazine* to highlight the tension between working moms and stay-at-home moms.[10] In 1990, *Newsweek* chronicled the shift from women fighting men in the 1970s with the women's movement, to mothers fighting mothers in the late 1980s into 1990.[11] At the time, 56 percent of mothers worked outside of the home, while 44 percent were stay-at-home moms. In a near fifty/fifty split, the mommy wars were a full-on battle.

And there's still been no cease-fire. The truth is, moms are tired. I know. I am one. Moms are weary of the pressure to live up to expectations and ideals that no human being could ever attain. Either we hear that our work at home is the pinnacle of greatness (leaving the mother who works outside of the home feeling inferior) or we hear that we are letting down women everywhere by staying home instead of taking advantage of the strides women have made in the workplace (leaving the mother who stays home feeling inferior). The mommy wars pit women against each other in a failed attempt to boost our pride over our own accomplishments. Instead of looking at our work through God's eyes, we look at it through our own—and wonder if we measure up.

Moms who stay home now are mostly doing so because of their own choice. But not all are.[12] Some are staying home because of the economic downturn, some because of the difficulty of juggling home life and work life, and others because of inflexible work schedules. What used to be a status symbol is now embedded with complex stories and life circumstances.

When we look at the mommy wars in the context of a culture that has far more moms choosing to stay home—not because of a lifelong ambition, as Story's research shows, but because of things like financial constraints, changes in perspective over a newborn baby, and pressures over work/life balance—it muddies the waters in our discussion about the value of at-home work itself. And it brings us back to the same questions our mothers and grandmothers had—questions about meaning and identity.

The Face of At-Home Work

Our search for meaning and identity has also led us to spend endless hours debating who's doing the at-home work—women or men. With the increase of mothers in the paid workforce, the percentage of stay-at-home moms has gone down from 49 percent in 1967 to 29 percent in 2012.[13] In families where Mom works outside of the home, some still sense the need for a parent, family member, or caretaker to be at home. Stay-at-home dads, though a small number, are growing. Current research says that 3.6 percent of at-home parents are dads.[14] At-home workers are not simply moms and dads, though. For households in which both parents work outside the home—either because of choice or necessity—grandparents, nannies, and at-home day-care workers are another group of people who spend their days in the mundane realities of childcare, housework, and creating order out of chaos.

Regardless of where we stand on who should be the face of at-home work, everyone is engaging in it on some level. My husband changes diapers. Sometimes he does laundry. We both clean up the same toys every night. My friend who is a nurse makes dinner for her kids at the end of the day. Her husband takes them to the doctor. They both help them brush their teeth and get ready for bed at night. There is no room for the mommy wars when your son gets sick in the middle of the night or your daughter needs an emergency trip to the dentist.

The majority of at-home work falls on the one who stays home, but it is for everyone. The mommy wars have no place in our discussion of at-home work because they distort it. They keep us fighting over the very work we are all doing, just in varying degrees. And in war we lose the value of the work that we all have some stake in. While we can spin our wheels endlessly debating who stays home, the reality is moms and dads everywhere wonder about the work itself. *Does it matter? Is it simply a way to survive? Is there something more to see in the dirty diapers, temper tantrums, dishwashing, and repetitive nature of housework?*

The Frazzled At-Home Worker

The "having it all" conversation, of course, doesn't help us answer these questions. The mommy wars planted the seed in our minds that we could have a growing career and family without missing a beat. While many are now debunking "having it all" as a myth, the impact on how we view at-home work still lingers. Far from giving us more freedom, the false promise of "having it all" has entrapped us even more. Now, women are expected to do everything—at-home work in the form of mommy bloggers, Pinterest boards, and child-centered living, plus work outside the home as well. Depending on our particular context, we either have a subculture that's telling us at-home work is our ultimate identity or one that's heaping disdain on the very nature of the work. In addition, we have a steady stream of television shows and networks (HGTV, Food Network), magazines (*Real Simple, Better Homes and Gardens*), and entertainment personalities (Martha Stewart, Rachael Ray) that glorify the work of the home, but that make it more about the business or consumption aspect of the work. In all this, we are losing sight of the work itself—why it matters and what purpose it serves.

In the 2011 movie *I Don't Know How She Does It*, stay-at-home moms are portrayed as privileged, judgmental women who spend their mornings at the gym and their afternoons dishing about school gossip, while the main character (an overworked professional mom) simply tries to remember what she is doing from day to day. She can hardly keep up with the work of her home, while her fellow moms who stay home can't find enough things to fill their mundane days. This portrayal of at-home work as an endless vacation for the brainless, wealthy white woman is not uncommon. A recent article even goes so far as to say that while at-home work is a gift and a privilege, it's hardly a job.[15] A job takes effort and skill; playing with your children all day does not. Again, with our consumption and leisure-focused society, we are missing the point of at-home work.

Even as I talk to my friends about their perceptions regarding at-home work, the ones who stay home are thankful for the opportunity, but wonder about it being on the same playing field as the careers they left behind. One friend confesses that she is reluctant to leave her work partly because she fears that she would get bored at home. Another says that, like the woman I met on the airplane, she doesn't know what she would do all day. It's simply too mundane.

Who hasn't wrestled with those issues? *Does at-home work really matter? Does it have value? Does it serve a greater purpose? Or is it too mundane? Too daily? Too frustrating? Too inefficient?*

Our answers to these questions don't come from pitting ourselves against one another in the mommy wars or endlessly debating who does the at-home work. It doesn't come from drawing firm lines about "separate spheres" and creating new technology to give us more free time.

The way forward to find meaning in at-home work is by seeing how it fits in the larger scheme of community, culture, and life. And that can be done only by going to the One who makes effective all that we do.

Finding Meaning in At-Home Work

Remember my conversation with the woman on the airplane? I struggled to talk with her about my work. This internal struggle is one I battle regularly when asked about what I do for a living. And while I didn't always aspire to the work I now do, I do enjoy it.

Like all major changes, my early days as a stay-at-home mom rocked me to the core. I had gone from days filled with fruitful conversations to days filled with crying and blank stares from two needy babies. Over time I began to see that being home had inherent value, but what I couldn't immediately see was how the work of the home had value as well. It was not merely about staying home to take care of the children (which made sense to my exhausted brain); I had to learn that there was value in the laundry and cleaning too.

To be honest, I'm still learning what it means to find purpose in these things. In a lot of ways, this book is born out of that internal struggle. The questions I asked myself in those early days of motherhood were no different from the questions I asked when I worked a job I found mundane and meaningless many years earlier. *What am I doing with my life? Does this matter? Can I have purpose if I'm not doing something great for God? Can I find meaning in the most mundane tasks? Can my work really be good if I don't always see it as good work?*

What I've learned is that God is glorified in the mundane work as much as he is in the magnificent. In fact, it is the mundane moments, the moments where we live each and every day, where we come to see the true greatness of God and his love for us. For most of my adult life I had been living for moments of grandeur, and when I transitioned to being primarily at home, I had to reconcile my deep aspirations for meaning and greatness in my work with a dirty microwave that needs cleaning and two babies that won't sleep through the night. Maybe you can relate. The culture tries to give at-home work meaning in our accomplishments or who has done the hardest thing, but honestly, most days the most spectacular thing we do is remember to brush our teeth or make the bed. Paul David Tripp says, "Our lives are comprised of 10,000 little moments and maybe only three or four dramatic ones."[16]

Doesn't that sound like at-home work to you? The work of the home is filled with thousands of little moments that make up our very existence. The kiss on a skinned knee, the special birthday meal for your daughter, the mopping of a floor that will only be walked on with muddy shoes as soon as your son gets home from soccer practice, the lesson about sharing after breaking up a sibling fight—all of these mundane moments shape a family and shape a culture. For all humans, when we engage with these little moments, we are imaging our Creator, who is the author of even the most mundane moments. For Christians, it's an even greater opportunity to increase the fame of Christ by becoming less, in the form of a servant (Matt. 20:26–28; John 3:30; Phil. 2:7). But it's not always as readily obvious to us as the more grandiose visions of Christianity and ambition we are accustomed to. While we appreciate at-home work, we—like many in our culture—have a hard time seeing it on the same playing field as the woman who manages an office or the man who operates on a dying patient.

But something profound is happening in the midst of our mundane at-home work. Such work is actually very God-like. Eugene Peterson, in the context of Psalm 121 says, "The same faith that works in the big things works in the little things. The God of Genesis 1 who brought light out of darkness is also the God of this day who guards you from every evil."[17] He is not just a God of big moments (like speaking the entire universe into existence or bringing dead people back to life). He is also a God of little moments (like protecting you from illness, providing unexpected income, and giving you food to sustain you). This should encourage us as we work in the seemingly mundane moments of working in our homes. God is working in the little moments, too.

This book is not going to give you the secret to being the best mom. But it is a book about the at-home work we do. The way our society thinks about this work is hardly biblical, whether we are trying to do it all, turning our nose up at it, or idolizing it. In order to find meaning and value in the mundane realities of at-home work, we are going to need to do some digging to find out the overarching meaning for our work as image bearers and the reason for the frequent disillusionment. That is where we are headed in the next chapter.

Getting Practical

My goal is for every chapter to apply specifically to real people in real situations. I hope to drive the point home that our work has value by seeing it through the life of another.

You will meet a variety of women at the end of each chapter. The three women here represent this changing face of at-home work.

Emily is a homeschooling mom of three. She also works for a small business part time from her home (as naps and sleeping children allow). Her mornings are spent juggling teaching her daughter the alphabet, helping her son with a math problem, and keeping her toddler entertained, all while trying to clean up from breakfast. Nap time and rest time usually allow her to recharge, prepare for dinner, respond to e-mail, or tackle any other household task that she is falling behind on (which lately feels like a lot). At night, after her kids are in bed, she pulls out her computer to start another type of work—bookkeeping.

Miriam is a stay-at-home mom of four. Her kids' ages vary from school age to an infant. Her days consist of getting the kids ready for school, preparing meals, folding laundry, helping with homework, playing with a toddler, and nursing a baby. She has a PhD in mathematics, so in order to bring in some extra income while her husband is in residency, she edits math journals. Even though she spends the majority of her time at home, she struggles to call herself a stay-at-home mom in the most traditional sense because she is bringing in some income.

Rachael is a teacher and mother of two. Like most working moms, she feels pulled in many directions. But there is one thing that is always waiting for her, even after that last paper is graded—the work of the home. From the bedtime stories to the dishes from the morning that she couldn't get finished, the work of the home is always waiting for her. She doesn't check her home responsibilities at the classroom. They follow her, and she often feels overwhelmed by it, but also is thankful for the time she gets with her daughters.

These women have more in common than the mommy wars lead us to believe. They are all contributing to the work of the home. They are the face of this changing at-home work. The work they are doing is good work, no matter how many hours a day they do it.

How has the changing face of at-home work changed the way you view your work? Do you value it more or less now?

2

Is There Life out There?

Growing up, one of my favorite singers was Reba McEntire. I spent hours belting out her songs with as much twang as I could muster as they blared from my cassette player. Back then, I hardly knew what I was singing. But after revisiting the familiar tunes, I now have a fresh understanding of the meaning of the lyrics of those songs I loved so much. In my youth, I didn't really get the message. As an adult, it comes across clearly.

One song in particular captures the feelings surrounding at-home work. "Is There Life Out There" tells the story of a wife and mom who married young and now wonders if there is something more for her than the life she now lives. As a wife and mom, she is consumed by the pressures of her home, and she is coming up short. The song is quick to say that she isn't interested in leaving—she just wonders what life is like on the other side.

Have you ever asked that question? At the end of a long day when you have yet to wash the peanut butter from lunch out of your hair, your son needs help with homework, the youth group is coming over, and the kitchen is full of dirty dishes, do you wonder if there is something better than the monotony of the work of the home? I know I have. Better yet, I remember that there *is* a life out there, one that seems to be far more fulfilling than what is happening within the walls of my own home.

Work is disillusioning, isn't it? All work (no matter how "high profile") is filled with the mundane, but there is something in particular about the work of the home that drives this point home (no pun intended). You fold laundry only to have it unfolded by a careless teenager who stuffs it in a drawer. You cook a beautiful meal only to have it devoured in seconds with little fanfare or praise. You pay bills only to have them arrive again at the same time next month. You rake leaves, and then a storm comes and blows your neighbor's leaves into your yard. Kids need help with their homework. Freshly painted walls get sticky fingerprints on them. The all-encompassing work of the home is one of many needs that seem to never be fully met.

A friend of mine is a nurse who works part time outside of the home. One of her fears about staying home full time is this feeling of meaninglessness that comes to us on our most boring days. *What if I just get so bored that I can't handle it?* she wonders. Another friend of mine asks the same question. She chooses to work part time solely because she doesn't think she can handle the mundane and ordinary parts of at-home work. She wants more than what (in her eyes) the work of the home offers.

The Original Intent of Work

As I've already said, all work is mundane on some level. We should realize this, right? One of my greatest regrets in my work before I had children is that I was unfaithful at work because I didn't like the boredom that often came with it. I didn't like my job, so I complained all of the time. I was bogged down with paperwork, so I checked Facebook every hour. I thought the work didn't matter, so I left before it was completed and refused to go the extra mile.

Work is hard. Work is boring. Work is cursed. But that's not how God intended it to be.

When God created Adam and Eve, he created them (*before* the fall) as workers in his garden (Gen. 1:28). As his image bearers, they were designed to work, create, and cultivate the world that he had made. Our role as workers is a function of our identity as image bearers (Gen. 1:27). You image God uniquely when you work. You tell a story to the world about his goodness and glory through your work. Regardless of how you might feel about it now, work is a good thing. And we were all made to do it. Tim Keller and Katherine Leary Alsdorf, in their book *Every Good Endeavor*, helpfully show how our work is designed to image God:

> We are called to stand in for God here in the world, exercising stewardship over the rest of creation in his place as his vice regents. We share in doing the things that God has done in creation—bringing order out of chaos, creatively building a civilization out of the material of physical and human nature, caring for all that God has made. This is a major part of what we were created to be. . . . Work has dignity because it is something that God does and because we do it in God's place, as his representatives.[1]

This means that work encompasses all of life. We work when we buy groceries and feed our hungry families. We work when we put a new ceiling fan in, providing cool air in warm summer

31

months. We work when we clean mold off a dirty shower curtain, making clean what was once filthy. We work when we educate our children, building future citizens in our society. We work when we teach our children about sharing, showing them that there are other people in this world beside themselves. We work when we fix a broken dishwasher, making new what was once destroyed. The people in our lives are loved and flourish by even the simplest of tasks that we do. God is glorified as we image him by bringing order of out chaos.

But work is more than just what we do—as Christians it is also how we love and worship God. Adam and Eve loved God by loving his creation through the cultivation of the ground, the care of the animals, and the multiplication of humanity. You and I also love God through our work. Whether we are picking up another round of antibiotics for a sick kid or winning a case in a courtroom, we love his world through the work we do every day.

In addition to loving vertically (loving God), we also were created to love horizontally (loving people) through our work. Our work is not only about our relationship to our Creator; it affects every other image bearer in this world. Work, as you will see in later chapters, is as much about the world as it is about the individual. We are relational beings, and every decision we make and vocation we perform is within the context of a relationship and community. Work originally was intended to reflect God, in whose image we were created, with love as a necessary, natural by-product.[2]

Throughout Scripture, we see people loving God and his creation through their work. Oholiab and Bezalel used their skills to design and create the various pieces of the tent of meeting, the mercy seat, and the ark of the testimony (Exodus 31). David was a shepherd (1 Sam. 16:11). Paul was able to travel all over, sharing the gospel while working as a tentmaker (Acts 18:3). And the Proverbs 31 woman, at the end of a book that talks about faithfulness in work being a by-product of wisdom, used all of her skills to love her family and her community.

The Curse on Work

But the inspiring call to and purpose of work isn't the end of the story. We know that within a few short chapters in Genesis, the perfect world that work was born into suddenly descended into chaos because of Adam and Eve's fateful choice. God tells Adam that painful toil, which wasn't present previously, will now mark his work (Gen. 3:17–19). Daily blessing through work is now fraught with daily hardship. Eve, who was intended to know only joy as she brought forth children into the world, will now know joy laced with pain (Gen. 3:16). Because of sin, work is no longer all that God intended it to be. Sure, we get glimpses of it, but all of it is marred by the effects of sin. Contrary to what many might think and feel, work itself is not a result of the fall. Its difficulty, however, is. Life in a post–Genesis 3 world is a mere shadow of the glorious beauty that God intended it to be.

This curse on work impacts our work at home, too. This is why we feel the pull to wonder if there is something else beyond the cycle of mundane tasks that we do every day. Groceries are expensive, and cooking is often done in the midst of other needs that demand to be met, robbing us of the joy of cooking's creative expression. Flowers die because of lack of rain or excessive heat, and sometimes the soil is just too rocky for anything to take root. Little children don't always want to sit still for story time. Older children don't always like to listen to us when we talk to them. Guests in our home aren't always grateful. The work that God gave us is made difficult by the stain of sin. We are marked by that stain every single day.

My husband and I like to compare the work of the home (and all work, really) to the meaninglessness portrayed in Ecclesiastes. When we pick up toys at the end of the day, knowing full well that they will be strewn about by toddlers in the morning, we stare at each other and say, "This, too, is chasing after the wind!" (see Eccles. 1:14). Don't you feel that way sometimes? The writer of Ecclesiastes knew this frustration well. He captures the feelings we all face when work is not all it is cracked up to be.

What about Compensation?

Another contributing factor to our disillusionment with at-home work is that we aren't paid for it. The work of the home used to be viewed as contributive work. Although the father might bring in income, the income was collective and for the entire family unit. The mother's work (and even the children's work) was seen as providing a way for the family unit to thrive. The father may have been a farmer or, post–Industrial Revolution, a factory worker, but all members of the family did their part to work. At times, the mother also provided income with her cooking, sewing, and homemaking skills. When work moved out of the home and into the marketplace, compensation became the driving marker of the value of work. The housewife of the 1950s was marked by the fact that she could afford to not make any money—not making money was a status symbol. To be able to stay home meant her husband made enough money for the both of them. Fast forward to our present day, and we are now defined by our salaries. The more money we make, the more successful we are perceived to be.

Julia, a part-time financial consultant with two small children, observes how the unique culture of New York City assigns an improper amount of dignity and worth to at-home work. Where she lives, a lot of the work of the home can be out-sourced. For eighty dollars a week, Julia pays someone to clean her two-bedroom apartment and wash and fold the household laundry. You can also hire someone to cook your meals for as little as one hundred and thirty dollars a week,[3] and groceries can be delivered straight to your apartment, sometimes even same-day for no additional cost.[4] Additionally, nannies are a common choice for childcare. In the business world, companies outsource certain jobs to save money in order to spend it on more valuable products and employees. Companies want the most return on their investment, so they spend less time and money on the tasks that will bring in less of a return or are considered not as highly skilled. We do the same thing when we outsource the work of the home. If it can be done cheaply or is too mundane, we are left with more money or time to spend on the things we value most. We have brought a business mind-set into the home. In our marketplace-driven society, where each job is assigned a monetary value, and especially in the financial-driven culture of New York City, Julia admits that there is a temptation to correlate the monetary compensation of a job to the dignity or worth of the job. How then might this correlation influence our attitudes toward those who stay home with their children and do the bulk of at-home work?

Of course, a variety of circumstances can lead us to use these services. This is not a commentary or judgment on the morality of having someone clean your home or having a nanny. But even for those who do take advantage of the opportunity, at the end of the day, the prominence of such services in our culture has shaped the way we think about at-home work and made it less valuable in our eyes.

It doesn't help that we have a string of television shows that only perpetuate the stereotype, from the *Real Housewives* franchise to *The Mindy Project*. At least in the case of *The Mindy Project*, the main character (Mindy) realizes that at-home work really is harder than we make it seem. And so does her fiancé (who, after thinking he could handle the work better than she did, realizes that it's hard work). More on this in chapter 7. But even with television shows attempting to crack stereotypes, some say that cultural ideas about at-home work have never been lower. Writing for *The Atlantic*, Wednesday Martin says:

> Sure, today's college-educated women have a degree of autonomy and self-determination that [Nora] Johnson and her peers only dreamed of, and that required an entire second wave of feminism to engineer, through consciousness raising, lawsuits, and legislation. Thanks to Title IX, they played sports that were off limits to a previous generation. Now, as middle- and upper-income women who stay home with kids they have recourse to no-fault divorce, laws protecting them from workplace discrimination, and access to birth control and abortion.
>
> And yet.
>
> The educated woman who stays home now may face a measure of not only the longing and lack of fulfillment that Johnson and [Betty] Friedan articulated, but also the awkward silence and turning away at a cocktail party—the lack of interest when she says she is a stay-at-home mother. She is in for a heaping helping of something relatively new: widespread cultural contempt.[5]

As Tim Keller says, our current culture's value on "knowledge" jobs (jobs where the main job requirement is the knowledge you bring to the job) also contributes to the devaluing of at-home work.[6] Even if you aren't a stay-at-home mom, nannies and housekeepers are not considered the most valuable contributors to a growing and cultured society. This goes back to the outsourcing idea. How do you feel about the factory worker in China who is making your electronics for you? Or the call center representative who is answering your call for technical support? To my shame, I can honestly say I don't think much of them. Work that is outsourced is viewed as expendable and the people more so. Our current mind-set is that if you aren't being compensated for your work, or if you aren't doing something that requires you to use your brain in the ways our society deems significant, the work is not truly work.

This idea is nothing new. The ancient Greeks placed great value on the mind, while the body and material world were for people of lesser value. Keller says that "work was a barrier to the highest kind of life" to the Greeks and that "the Greeks understood that life in the world required work, but they believed that not all work was created equal."[7] This same sort of ideology was prevalent during the Reformation, too. The cloistered life, where one prayed, studied, and served God in solitude, was of great spiritual value. Ordinary laborers were a lower class of people. While it might seem that we are in a new frontier regarding how we value (and devalue) work, we are simply continuing the cycle that has been spinning for centuries. It just has new packaging.

But if the work of the home is still needed (and who doesn't need clean underwear, dinner every night, and well-adjusted children?), how do we quantify it if it no longer falls under income earned and a paycheck deposited? Every so often, a major media outlet reports on how much money a stay-at-home mom would actually earn if she we were paid for her work and hours on the job. In 2011, *Forbes* reported that stay-at-home moms should be paid $115,000 a year for the work they do because it comprises so many different jobs.[8] But I think these conversations are misplaced, because they reflect our view of the home as being a place of consumption rather than a place of productivity. When productivity and work moved outside of the home, income became personal and not collective. But a recovery of seeing the home as a place for the family's productivity, and as part of the common good of society, helps reorient our perspective on the pay for at-home work, along with our purpose in our work. Even if you outsource some of the at-home work, you can still appreciate and value the work being done by seeing it as part of the all-encompassing purpose of the home.

One way my husband and I try to combat the tendency to pit one work against the other is by not making a distinction between at-home work and work outside of the home. When someone asks where I work, we say, "The home." While I bring in some money through writing projects, he is the primary wage earner. But we view my work at home as a vital contribution, even if I never receive a paycheck for it. We have one family income, and we all do our part to help our family thrive. And while I am the primary parent at home, he also contributes to the overall work of the home in a variety of ways. We are all working together for the good of our family, sometimes for compensation and sometimes not. There is a lot of give-and-take for both of us, even if the work in the home isn't split fifty-fifty. Regardless, all of our work has value. In some small way, we hope our perspective on the collective income moves us toward the recovery of the notion that our home should be a place of productivity, rather than endless amounts of consumption.

We hope to model for our children, and those around us, that everyone in our family is working because that is what we were made for. And all of our work matters.

It's not just in how you talk with your spouse about at-home work that can contribute to how you and I value the work. Our children are listening and watching how we value the work of the home as well. In an effort to teach her children that work is contribution, including at-home work, author Jen Wilkin and her husband were intentional about how they assigned chores and compensated (or didn't compensate) for them, with this end goal in mind:

> As those whose work is ultimately done for the glory of God, we ask, "How much can I contribute?" before we concern ourselves with "How much will I receive?" Think how differently the world would function if everyone regarded work through this lens.
>
> This is why in our home we didn't tie allowance (compensation) to chores (work). Instead, we explained to the kids that their contributions to the upkeep of domestic order were absolutely essential. We were not merely trying to train them to obey or to be responsible, we actually needed them to share the burden of work for our family to flourish.[9]

I'm not saying that giving allowances is wrong. And I'm not saying that compensation in the marketplace does not matter. In my effort to bring value to the unpaid work of the home, I don't want to diminish the need to pay people a fair wage for the work they do. But it is important for us to see work as a contribution, and not always with a dollar sign attached to it. We must walk a fine line between valuing unpaid work and providing people with the compensation they deserve for their work.

Missing the Point

I believe that our feelings of meaninglessness and our culture's misunderstanding regarding compensation are exercises in missing the point. In fact, they only contribute to how we feel about the mundane realities of our work. Add this to the pressures of an Internet-obsessed world, where every perfect birthday party, every clean bathroom, and every gourmet meal is displayed for all to see, and it is no wonder we question whether we are doing enough in our work—or even doing work at all.

If we are going to recover a theology of at-home work and truly understand our purpose in it, we have to further explore two key ways that we misunderstand work:

1. Work must be paid to be meaningful.
2. Work must accomplish something great to be meaningful.

As I've already said, when we talk about work *only* in terms of compensation or talk about it *only* in terms of accomplishing grandiose things, then we miss the point of our work completely. You and I were made to work as a function of our role as image bearers. Work is not simply about closing a business deal, teaching a class full of children, or discovering a new treatment for a disease. It is also about loving and serving our neighbor.[10]

An even more troubling aspect of our culture's understanding of work is that we tend to think that if our work doesn't accomplish something big, it's not worth our time.

But we are defining big and important by the wrong scale. The Bible reminds us that the last will be first and the first will be last (Matt. 19:30; 20:16). Jesus tells us that it's not great faith that we need in order to move mountains; it is faith as small as a mustard seed (Luke 17:6). God chooses the weak things to shame the wise (1 Cor. 1:18–31). He even chooses an instrument of torture and death to bring about the salvation of broken sinners like you and me. Ordinary and mundane is the way of Christ.

Michael Horton challenges us in our restlessness in the ordinary:

> Given the dominance of The Next Big Thing in our society, it is not at all surprising that the Christian subculture is passionate about superlatives. Many of us were raised in a Christian subculture of managed expectations, called to change ourselves or our world, with measurable results. There always had to be a cause du jour to justify our engagement. Otherwise, life in the church would simply be too ordinary. Like every other area of life, we have come to believe that growth in Christ—as individuals or as churches—can and should be programmed to generate predictable outcomes that are unrealistic and are not even justified biblically. We want big results—sooner rather than later. And we've forgotten that God showers his extraordinary gifts through ordinary means of grace, loves us through ordinary fellow image bearers, and sends us into the world to love and serve others in ordinary callings.[11]

In our Christian circles, we are tempted by this pull toward the spectacular. Ordinary exercises in faithfulness regarding our work don't cut it in a culture that is looking for the next big Internet sensation or viral video. If it's not funny, it's not worth sharing. If it's not tweet worthy, it's not worth talking about. If it's not saving a faraway village for Jesus, it's not worth our investment. We are living in a time when being ordinary is the worst thing that can happen to a person, and nothing screams ordinary like at-home work. Few people see the daily work that you do. Unless you raise the next president, celebrity, or athlete, few people will praise you at the city gates for the work that you have put in over the years. We all feel a strong desire (both from inside us and from the culture) to do something radical with our life, to not waste it. And sometimes it feels wasteful to spend your life on at-home work.

But that's not the way God views your work. He sees your work and delights in it. God cares about what happens behind the closed doors of your house each and every day because he cares about the people in it. He cares about the seemingly ordinary work that you do because he is the One who created you for the very work you are doing right now.

It's not just this pull toward the meaningful that causes us to miss the point in our work. Maybe you don't feel like you need to make a name for yourself. You have always wanted to stay home with your children. You never wanted any other job—and now you are doing it and feel complete. But do your feelings about your day rise and fall with every task accomplished or with happy children who don't throw their food on the floor or throw tantrums at bedtime? While you may not be tempted to brush off your at-home work as unimportant, disillusionment may come in the temptation to define yourself by the work at home. Do these thoughts resonate with you? *The more I do, the better I feel. I'm better than her because I stay home with my kids.* My concern with this view of at-home work is that it tends to overcompensate for the culture's view of at-home work. If the world can't value it, we will. Unfortunately, sometimes we swing that pendulum too far. And this has devastating consequences for our spiritual life (as we will see in coming chapters).

There is a middle road for all of us—those who devalue the work of the home and those who idolize it. Understanding God's original intent for our work, what happened to our work when sin entered the world, and how we miss the point in our work is the first step. Your daily work matters, friend. Whether it feels like meaningful work or not, I assure you it is. And I hope in the coming chapters to show you just how much you are imaging your loving Creator when you faithfully labor in your daily work in the home.

Getting Practical

Tovey is a stay-at-home mom to three children living in New York City. She is confronted with the culture's view of at-home work almost everywhere she goes. Recently, she ran into a friend who seemed a bit surprised that she had another kid (her third). This friend, an unbeliever and single, couldn't believe someone would put herself through having another baby, not to mention stay home with her children all day long. When she expressed her shock at Tovey's life, Tovey smiled and commiserated that it really was backbreaking work and as hard as her friend perceived it to be. Tovey told me that she was quick to lightheartedly agree with her friend when she implied that she was nuts for choosing to do something so hard (a third time), instead of emphasizing that the work she does is meaningful and important—hard as it may be.

Often when we present at-home work, we talk about the disheveled mom, the mess on the floor, the fact that you no longer feel like a human being. But when we do that, as Tovey says, we end up perpetuating the bad reputation our at-home work gets. It's maligned because we let it be maligned. When people tell us it is too hard, we grin and bear it. But we would never expect the same response from someone who has a difficult job outside the home (like a doctor in residency or a teacher, for example). Those are noble professions. They require hard work, but it's so worth it, we think. "Aren't all valuable things hard?" Tovey says. "There is this view regarding at-home work that you should either be complaining about how hard it is all of the time or you should love it and never talk about the difficulty. But that doesn't help anyone."

Tovey has also experienced our cultural disdain for ordinary work. "Our culture tells us that the goal of life is to get a job where you don't have to do grunt work, but at-home work is grunt work," she told me. We turn our noses up at people who work at Walmart or as janitors their entire lives, yet menial tasks are what make up the day of the average mom who works at home.

Tovey's experience reminds us that even how we talk about our at-home work with others can contribute to our disillusionment with it. How does the way you talk about your work contribute to your disillusionment with it? Do you complain to your friends about it? How has the curse of sin impacted your understanding of your work?

3

What about the Chores?

You might have heard the saying "Everyone wants a revolution. Nobody wants to do the dishes."[1] I don't know about you, but I can relate to that. I'm all about revolutions, greatness, and saving people in Jesus's name, but dishes? Laundry? Cleaning the bathrooms? Those tasks hardly feel like the mountaintop experiences I have longed for since I started dreaming big things.

And yet, those very tasks are what make up my day—along with picking up trucks and trains, cooking meals, grocery shopping, and sweeping and mopping the floor (among other things). The general work of homemaking is what I spend the bulk of my time doing in my season of life. But even when my work wasn't primarily in the home, the dishes still needed to be done, the bed needed to be made, and we needed to eat—every day. From the time my mom first taught me how to clean the bathrooms as a kid until now, the daily upkeep of the home has been part of my life. I imagine it has been part of yours, too.

How It Used to Be

As we saw in chapter 1, the home shifted from a place of productivity to one of personal identity in the 1950s. Women defined themselves as homemakers or housewives, and advertisers targeted a middle-class woman's desire for a perfect home.

An ad for vitamins meant to give a housewife energy features a conversation between the husband and wife that goes like this:

> Husband: Gosh, honey, you seem to thrive on cooking, cleaning and dusting—and I'm all tuckered out by closing time. What's the answer?
>
> Wife: Vitamins, Darling! I always get my vitamins.
>
> And then the slogan: *So the harder a wife works, the cuter she looks.*

A Christmas advertisement shows a wife joyfully admiring her new vacuum cleaner with the statement: *Christmas morning she will be happier with a Hoover.*[2]

Advertisers played to the cultural expectation that to stay at home was to be a good housewife. And to be a good housewife was to keep your home perfectly clean and ready for your husband when he came home from his job. I will cover this more in the next chapter, but while you and I don't see as much of this in advertising today, we do see a greater emphasis on the at-home work being about the children and caring for children in the best way possible.

Although we still see advertisements that promise clean floors, spotless bathrooms, and spot-free dishes, much of the focus has now moved to parenting rather than the upkeep of the home. The major selling point of a current advertisement for frozen meals (a big development that shifted work out of the home) is that if you buy the frozen dinner, the frozen chicken tenders, or any other frozen product offered by this company, then you will have time to do what really matters—driving your daughter to soccer practice, attending a piano recital, or reading to your kindergartner. With the amount of activities that children are involved in and the busyness of life in general, most of us are struggling to empty the dishwasher or fold the piles of clean laundry that build up on our beds. Among women I know (myself included), the general consensus is that the physical work of the home (the laundry, cooking, dishes, mopping, and sweeping, etc.) are secondary and optional. We joke about the home being a wreck, even judging the one who (somehow) is able to keep the home remarkably clean. Many of us wouldn't dream of leaving the children to play at the park alone, but we are probably okay with a ring around the toilet. One (the children) speaks to our identity in the home, the other (the toilet), not so much.

Some "mommy blogger" sites are devoted to encouraging moms that the chaos of their homes is perfectly normal, and it is the woman with the clean home who is strange. I'll admit I've found myself nodding right along with statements like this one:

> My oldest son has never seen us use the shower in our master bath. He's four. We need to replace the tile and just haven't managed somehow. I thought this was horrible, abnormal, horrific shame until, in flagrant disregard for social mores, I mentioned this to other mothers. Two of them copped to unusable bathrooms. One mentioned a deck with holes. Another has to warn visitors not to attempt the front stairs. I salute you, my sisters in disorder.[3]

The author of this post, like many moms, feels the pull to have a perfect home, yet also the desire to take care of her kids. So she wrote an honest piece about how some moms can keep a home in order and others can't—and it's all perfectly normal.

Even if you don't have disdain for the clean homes around you, if you're honest you'll likely admit that at times keeping up with the housework is simply too much. Carla confessed to me that with two young children it is just hard to keep things orderly in her home like she would like to. Riddled with self-imposed expectations (not to mention Pinterest expectations), she finally had to yield to reality—even her best efforts to keep things orderly find their match in a two-year-old who dumps his toys right after she picks them up.

The physical work of cleaning a home is not what we think about when we think of the home as being valuable. The kids are. Of course, human beings have more value than a clean kitchen. I think that's what the culture of the housewife got wrong. It does us no good if our house is in perfect condition and our children are ignored or people aren't welcomed and cherished when they come into our home. And there are seasons of life that warrant putting these things aside. I know this firsthand. As I'm writing this chapter, I have a four-month-old baby and twin toddlers. Life in a post–Genesis 3 world means I can't get all of the work done. Maybe you are beyond the little-kids years, but with all of the extracurricular activities, school projects, and church responsibilities you find yourself wishing you had margin for the housework, too. Or maybe you are a single mother, and between your job in the office and your job at home, you wish there were more time in the day. Something always needs to be cleaned, fixed, cooked, or organized. You and I will not have perfect homes in this life. We can't get it all done (more on that later). And even when we clean something or cook something, all too often there is little to show for it in the immediate aftermath. So please don't hear me saying that your house must be perfect. I know mine isn't. But let's consider for this chapter why the physical work of the home does in fact matter, even if all you do today is make grilled cheese sandwiches.

First we need to see how the physical work of the home has been devalued. Once we understand what bogs us down, we can move into why the "chores" matter. I've divided the physical work of the home into three sections: the ordinary chores (laundry, cleaning, etc.), cooking and eating, and decorating. In each of these sections we are going to look at God's creative intention for this work, how sin tangibly impacts it, and how Christ gives us a redeemed perspective on it.

You Do What?

While being called a housewife might not be popular now (unless you are part of a reality television show), our culture doesn't view housekeeping as a valuable profession either. You don't go to school to learn how to clean the house. You don't take classes in ironing or folding clothes. Cooking classes are designed for those who want to start a restaurant, not those who want to feed a family. With the shift that happened in the '60s, where the work of the home became less valuable (and more about the people in the home), the work itself didn't just disappear. The work still had to be done, so it was outsourced—and seen as beneath educated people. Women would hire housekeepers to clean their homes and care for their children, while they kept up the status of an affluent housewife. Even the absence of home economics courses in schools indicates that we view housework as irrelevant to getting ahead in the world. We live in a society that doesn't value ordinary work, and at-home work falls into that category.

My dad has been in the window cleaning business since I was a little girl. What started as a job to provide for his family while he was in seminary has become a trade he can take anywhere. Now he owns a window cleaning business in Florida, while also serving as a pastor. My dad spends his days with his hands in dirty, soapy water, cleaning the windows of homes and businesses. This is hardly viewed as a job for educated and wealthy people. I remember the crushing words at the school lunch table as a girl mocked the fact that my daddy washed people's house windows for a living. I fought back tears as I listened to her talk about her dad's important corporate job, and in that moment, I was confronted for the first time with an understanding of work that I had never thought of before, and have only recently started thinking about again. My dad has had his fair share of comments about his work from people who see him washing windows in the hot sun. One woman looked at her son as they walked past my dad and said, "And *that* is why you go to college."

This faulty thinking is not uncommon. We don't see the more menial jobs as being as important as the jobs that require a college degree. But God created us to work, not just be college educated (though that is not a bad thing!). Part of the reason we struggle so much with the work of the home is because, as Tim Keller says, we put a greater emphasis in our culture on the "knowledge" jobs instead of embracing the dignity of all work.[4]

It's easy to see at-home work as insignificant, even beneath educated people. But the truth is that there is so much more to the work that you are doing than you realize. Author Kathleen Norris talks about God's powerful presence in the mundane details of our days, even through our work:

> The Bible is full of evidence that God's attention is indeed fixed on the little things. But this is not because God is a Great Cosmic Cop, eager to catch us in minor transgressions, but simply because God loves us—loves us so much

that the divine presence is revealed even in the meaningless workings of daily life. It is in the ordinary, the here-and-now that God asks us to recognize that the creation is indeed refreshed like dew-laden grass that is "renewed in the morning" (Ps. 90:5), or to put it in more personal and theological terms, "our inner being is renewed every day" (2 Cor. 4:16). Seen in this light, what strikes any modern readers as the ludicrous attention to detail in the book of Leviticus, involving God in the minutiae of daily life—all the cooking and cleaning of a people's domestic life—might be revisioned as the very love of God. A God who cares so much to be present to us in everything we do.[5]

Another way to think of God being hidden in our work is to say that we are imaging God as we work. You and I were created to work because God himself works. It is a function of being image bearers. Everything we do, whether it is work in the home or outside of the home, is imaging the God who made us to work.

Imaging God in Ordinary Chores

So in light of God being part of the work that we do, being hidden in the work that we do, how do we as image bearers image him in such ordinary tasks as housework? How does working out the grass stain in your son's baseball pants or shampooing the carpet image God? The work of the home is nothing to be ashamed of. It is valuable, important work. It is necessary work. It is work that God sees as integral to his work in this world. In fact, because you bear his image, you are imaging him with every task you accomplish in your home on any given day. A task that does this clearly is when you bring order out of chaos. Let's think for a moment about how you, as a created being, bring order out of chaos in your work.

You take a room that is cluttered and in disarray and organize it and declutter. Order out of chaos. You clean and disinfect a refrigerator that is growing things that are hardly edible. Order out of chaos. You sort, pretreat, wash, fold, and put away piles of laundry. Order out of chaos.

With every ordinary task you do, you are bringing order into this chaotic world that we live in. While it might feel hardly God-like, I assure you that it is.

God, staring at the vastness of time and space, spoke creation into existence out of nothing (Gen. 1:1–3). God quiets storms to a whisper (Ps. 107:29). And most of all, God in the flesh brings order to our chaotic souls by dying on the cross and giving us his righteousness.

You also image him when you care for the details of your home. As God cares for the seemingly mundane details of creation, so you care for the seemingly mundane details of a home that needs to be kept in order. How does God care for creation? By watering the plants with rain, by providing gardeners and farmers to work the land, by bringing forth fruit in season (Psalm 1), by caring for animals (Matt. 6:26), and by giving us our daily bread (Ps. 78:23–25; Matt. 6:11; Luke 11:3). As his image bearers, we are part of this creation care. While God at times cares for his creation in spectacular ways, like causing a drought to cease through unexpected rain, more often he cares for creation through you and me, and more specifically for our purposes, through the work of the home.

This point was illuminated to me when we recently let our youngest son crawl around on our deck, which desperately needs to be cleaned up and stained. We knew the wood was old and dry, but we hadn't gotten around to fixing it. As I was putting him to bed that night, I realized there were dozens of tiny splinters in his little feet. Of course, we started looking into having our deck refinished immediately! But while restaining our deck will make it more pleasing to the eye, it will also protect all of our kids from splinters when they play on it. We don't always think about a stained deck, or any mundane task, as God's means of caring for his creation, but this seemingly ordinary task cares for the world and the people he has made. And I'm sure you can think of examples throughout your own day that seem so ordinary, yet in God's eyes are precious and meaningful to his created beings.

But even when we understand how doing daily chores images God, we see that our work doesn't always get done smoothly and easily. Life in a fallen world means bad things happen when the work doesn't get done. Life in a fallen world means thorns and thistles get in the way of finishing our daily chores. Our backyard regularly floods, leaving it uninhabitable for a garden or even grass. Mold grows in refrigerators. Last night's dinner is caked on dishes in the sink. And in our sin we don't always have eyes to see how our work is doing God's work of bringing order out of chaos or caring for his creation. Frankly, it just feels too mundane most days to be that grandiose. In a lot of ways these feelings of insignificance over the ordinary chores is the most devastating effect of sin on our work. Because we live in a culture that prizes the more physical aspects of the work of the home the least (over caring for children and even decorating), we feel the sinful devaluing of it acutely. It's harder to see a clean cabinet as valuable when it's not as culturally acceptable as signing your kid up for music lessons.

This is all owing to the curse, isn't it? We take the good things that God has given us (work, the home, etc.) and make them seem pointless. But for those in Christ, the futility of the ordinary chores isn't the end of the story.

Our work is meant to be a means of loving God through loving our neighbors, so the greatest love we can show them (even the neighbors in our own home) is to bring some sense of order in a broken and chaotic world. Sometimes this looks like opening your home to a friend who is weary, and sometimes it looks like disinfecting the whole house after a stomach bug makes its way through.

Tim Keller says that this work of bringing order out of chaos is a continuation of God's plan for us to rule and subdue the earth (more on this in chap. 8). We take the raw materials available to us (dish soap, clean hand towels, mops, brooms, storage bins), grab hold of the unruly clutter and mess of our homes, and bring it under our orderly care. We are imaging God by our work through obeying the creation mandate that still leads us today. Keller writes:

> Whenever we bring order out of chaos, whenever we draw out creative potential, whenever we elaborate and "unfold" creation beyond where it was when we found it, we are following God's pattern of creative cultural development.[6]

Every time you pick up toys after a day full of play or when you mow grass that has gotten unruly because of the warmth and moisture of summer, you are bringing order out of chaos. You are pushing back the forces of darkness by even such small measures as cleaning up the family desk in the kitchen by saying that chaos and disorder will not reign forever. You are imaging your Creator by making something out of nothing, by making clean what was once filthy, and by making broken things new.

Imaging God in Cooking and Eating[7]

Food is such a popular topic. In fact, food is so popular right now that it gets an entire channel devoted to it—the Food Network (decorating and home improvement get channels too—more on that in the next section). Cooking and eating are ingrained in us as image bearers. God created human beings (and animals) with a need for sustenance through food, and then he made that food for them (Gen 1:29–30).

God has directly provided nourishment for his people since creation. He rained manna and quail from the sky (Exodus 16). He brought the Israelites to the "land flowing with milk and honey" (Ex. 3:8, 17; 33:3). But he's also provided food for his people through others. Boaz provided for Ruth (Ruth 2:14–18). The widow of Zarephath fed Elijah by the hand of God (1 Kings 17:7–16). In the New Testament we see the declaration of Jesus's deity through how he made abundant food out of very little (Matt. 14:13–21; Mark 6:30–44) and turned water into wine (John 2:1–11). Sometimes God provides miraculously by raining food from the sky or turning little into much, but more often than not he provides for people through others. We are part of that provision.

Consider a family meal. Maybe you have other guests around your table, or maybe it is just your family, but you have spent the bulk of the afternoon chopping vegetables, thawing meat, preparing a casserole, baking a dessert, and warming bread. As your belly growls with hunger and your children run into the kitchen begging for food, you gather them all together, sit down, and thank God for his provision of food. It's a standard prayer, isn't it? *Thank you, God, for providing this meal for us.* But did it magically appear on your table? You know better than anyone that it did not. *You* made it. You were even the one who bought the groceries for the meal. Yet you thank God for his fatherly care in giving you your daily bread. As an image bearer, you image God by providing for the people at your table. When you open up your kitchen and table for others, you are part of God's provision for the people he has created.

Let's take this example to an even more personal level. Women understand acutely what it means to provide physically for the sustenance of others. Throughout the writing of this book, I have been nursing my third baby. The Bible actually is not silent on how we image God through feeding our babies. Isaiah reminds us that if we know that a woman won't forget her nursing baby, how much more will God not forget his own (Isa. 49:15)? Women uniquely image God by their ability to not only bring forth life through childbirth, but also through their ability to sustain life with their bodies. David tells us in Psalm 22 that one evidence of God's past, present, and future faithfulness to him is that he learned to trust God even at his mother's breast (Ps. 22:9). Babies don't need to be taught to trust that food will come. They simply receive it with eagerness. And we learn from them (and ourselves) that God is a God who will meet all of our needs.

But even a cursory look at the world around us reveals that this is not always the case. Depending on your financial circumstances, sometimes it is cost prohibitive to even make a family meal, or have people in your home to share the meal with you. The delight that food was intended to provide for us, the comfort cooking was intended to give to those who partook of the meal, and the community that was supposed to be forged through eating often elude us. We aren't always able to see the worshipful, God-imaging nature of our cooking and eating. And what about problems that come with nursing? We live in a post–Genesis 3 world, where the curse on our work and on our ability to sustain life is still rearing its ugly head. So while we can acknowledge what our cooking and eating were meant to be for people as we image God, we know that it is tragically marred by sin.

Again, sin has radically distorted every good thing that God made, even food. For some, it manifests as an eating disorder that prevents you from eating with others. Others obsess over eating the newest healthy food or the latest fad diet that keeps you from enjoying the food in front of you. Maybe you are burdened with a food-related allergy or illness and you long for the days of carefree cooking and consuming. Maybe you have a condition that prevents you from nursing your baby no matter what you try. Or maybe your problems with food are just owing to lack of time. You remember the days when you could leisurely prepare a meal for yourself or someone else, and now you are scrambling to get something on the table before soccer practice starts. Many things keep us from seeing God's hand in our work in the kitchen. And while I can't add more hours to your day or remove illnesses or disorders, I can try to point you to God's transforming work in how we see our cooking and eating.

Rachel Jankovic says:

> Jesus came into the world "eating and drinking" (Mt. 11:19). Far from coming to deliver a series of lectures, Jesus came to feed us, to eat with us, to save us. Jesus came to partake with us. But He didn't come just to partake with us and then leave us as we were. He came to eat with us, to invite us into fellowship with Him, and to transform us through that fellowship.[8]

So much of Jesus's earthly ministry happened in the context of food and homes. He spent time in the homes of Mary, Martha, and Zacchaeus (Luke 10:38–42; 19:1–10). He ate with the disciples (Matt. 9:10; 12:1; 14:19; 26:26–27; Luke 24:41–43). The table of fellowship that Jesus offered was an integral part of his earthly ministry, almost as if to say, "I'm here, and I'm making all things new." He ministered through the ordinary, mundane reality of the home. This has tremendous implications for us as his followers. Because he came, lived, died, and conquered sin and death, we have hope in this broken world. It's not perfect yet, but we can still work with what we have because Jesus died to make all things new.

But it is not just his earthly ministry that gives us hope for a coming restoration in the kitchen. Jesus also is going to eat with us in the new heavens and the new earth (Rev. 19:6–9). The marriage supper of the Lamb is the feast of all feasts, where there are no dietary restrictions, disordered eating, or budgets that can't afford the grocery store run. Just feasting. And we won't be the ones making the food then; we will be fed by the One who is the "bread of life," who is making all things new, even our work in cooking and feeding hungry people.

Imaging God in Creating Beauty

The work of the home is not just about chores and feeding people, though. Our physical labors in the home are also an attempt to make things beautiful. When God created the world, he declared it good (Gen. 1:31). There is beauty in his creation. We have a row of crape myrtle trees in our backyard. I don't know the first thing about planting or caring for trees, plants, or anything garden related, but the previous owners of our home must have planted these trees. They bloom every year with little to no effort on our part, and I never tire of admiring their beauty. The pink flowers stand out against the green of our backyard, and it is a beautiful sight to see. God created them. He made soil to nourish them. God gave me eyes to admire their beauty. And I get to experience and appreciate their beauty. God cares about the beautiful. In our work of caring for his creation through the physical work of the home, we are given an opportunity to create beauty for our enjoyment and for his glory.

Edith Schaeffer in *The Hidden Art of Homemaking* says that Christians recognize that in creating a beautiful space, they are in turn reflecting the God who makes all things beautiful:

> Surely each person who lives in an "interior" of any sort should realize that "Interior Decoration" is the first opportunity to bring forth "Hidden Art," in some small measure. And for the Christian who is consciously in communication with the Creator, surely his home should reflect something of the artistry, the beauty and order of the One whom he is representing, and in whose image he has been made![9]

Christians, Schaeffer says, should have the most beautiful spaces because they understand that God delights in beauty and is the author of beauty.[10] We apply this logic often to things like art, but it can be applied to the home as well. This does not mean that our homes become a function of our personal identity or rise to the often idolatrous standards of HGTV and *Southern Living* (hardly a biblical ideal). Rather, it means that in our efforts to care for the home, we must not dismiss the value that beauty and creative expression bring to the table. Every home will look different because every person is different. We all express and create in varying degrees and with different abilities. And our standard of beauty is often different from God's standard. Perfection is not the standard. Making things beautiful for the good of others is the standard. In our day, we have made the home a function of our identity, largely exacerbated by a social media culture that provides an outlet for us to put our best foot forward at all times. But I want to reclaim a biblical understanding of beauty for us. Not so that we can garner "likes" on Instagram or "pins" on Pinterest. We want God to get the glory and people to feel loved. The curse makes us want to glory in our beautification efforts. But a redeemed heart points to the beautiful Redeemer.

Go back to the purpose of the home. What is it? Love God and love neighbors. You love others by allowing your home to be a refuge, a place where people feel loved and welcomed. Remember Carla, who struggles to find time to get all of the physical work of the home done. It's hard in her season of life to get this work done, but she does find time for something of great importance. "Even though I can't get a lot of cleaning and housework done these days," she told me, "I do want my home to be a refuge for my kids. I want to make this a safe environment for them." Every person who steps into our home, whether it is our spouse, our kids, our next-door neighbor, or a church member, should get a sense of welcome and care. God welcomes us into his family (Rom. 15:7), he is preparing a beautiful home for us (John 14:2–4), and he is the beautiful One (Isa. 4:2; 33:17). Our decorating efforts should reflect these realities.

This is what Schaeffer is getting at. Everyone creates beauty in different ways. Every home takes on the feel of its owner. An urban home with limited space looks different from a country home with forty acres. But the principle remains—the work of the home creates a safe refuge for all who walk through our doors.

Decorating a home looks different for everyone, but it does matter. While I do like to decorate my home, I approach this topic as one who is not particularly gifted at color palettes and room organization. It takes effort on my part. My sister-in-law, however, can look at a room and tell you what will work in that space. She can rearrange furniture in ways I never would think of, and when she helps me think through these things, it makes our house more inviting and comfortable for guests and family. We want people to come into our homes and feel welcomed and loved. By making order out of chaos, caring for creation, valuing cooking, and desiring beauty in its myriad and unique forms, we can do just that for people in our ordinary, everyday work.

But the home is not just about the tasks that need to get done. The home is about the people who live in it too. And that is where we are headed in the next chapter.

Getting Practical

Megan's husband loves biscuits. I mean, who doesn't? But biscuits can be hard to make, especially if you like the fluffy kind. A few years ago a woman in her church, who is a biscuit pro, invited Megan over to teach her how to make biscuits. One afternoon this woman gave her time, her kitchen, and her knowledge to Megan, so Megan could turn around and bless her husband with biscuits. Megan made biscuits not for herself, but for her husband. She used her time, her hands, and her willing spirit to learn the craft of making biscuits so her husband could enjoy a good biscuit. This is what the everyday chores of the home are all about—giving our time, energy, and creativity for the good of others. Cooking biscuits is not just for the joy of the one who is cooking. The people who will consume them matter as well, and are blessed by the loving effort to provide them.

Maybe it's not biscuits in your house, but everyone has something that they love, that they enjoy, that makes them feel appreciated. Is it a clean toilet? A favorite breakfast sandwich? An organized desk? Fresh flowers from the farmer's market? How does your work, like Megan's biscuit-baking afternoon, serve the people in your home?

4

My Home, My People

I heard someone say once that laundry is not something you do, but it is a state of being. At the time of this writing, I have three kids, ages three and under, so in a house with five messy people, that statement could not be truer. I have five freshly washed loads of laundry sitting next to the folded, but not put away, laundry from five days ago to prove it. You might get laundry in its proper place more quickly than I do, but I'm guessing you resonate with the fact that laundry is just one of the things required of us in our work. As I said in the last chapter, the physical work of the home is constant, but it's not all housework. Our work is not just about washed windows, fresh bed sheets, grocery shopping, and a clean oven. We are not glorified housekeepers. There are *people* that fill the rooms of our homes too. The work of the home is as much about the people inside the home as it is the physical work itself. And we are constantly moving between the two—folding laundry then helping with a math problem, right?

Who hasn't been there? You are caught between a question

about the school play and a boiling pot of water for dinner. You see the floor that needs the milk wiped up from breakfast, but you also see the husband who needs to talk about his plans for the day. You have to buy groceries, but you also have to pick up your grandkids from school. You are scheduled to deliver a meal to a friend who had surgery, but you have no clean dishes to cook with. The work of the home involves a seemingly endless tension between the people who fill it and the physical work those people create for us. Some of this is just the reality of life, but it's also a result of a shift in how we view at-home work.

Two Competing Jobs

As the physical labor of the home became easier, and as children became less necessary for the sustenance of a family unit, children became a protected class and were no longer seen as contributors. In a post–World War II world, everyone had more time on their hands. The more our work moved outside of the home, the more time children had to play outside, take up sports and hobbies, and hang around the home leisurely. Couple that with the growing change in how the work of the home is classified—*stay-at-home mom* versus *homemaker*—and it is no wonder we feel this tension. Jennifer Senior has documented this shift in her book, *All Joy and No Fun*, where she says:

> Today parents pour more capital—both emotional and literal—into their children than ever before, and they're spending longer, more concentrated hours with their children than they did when the work-day ended at five o'clock and the majority of women still stayed home. Yet parents don't know what it is they're supposed to *do*, precisely, in their new jobs. "Parenting" may have become its own activity (its own profession, so to speak), but its goals are far from clear.[1]

I'll share more about guilt over what we do in chapter 7, but we do feel this tension, don't we? As at-home work shifted in its emphasis, children became the focal point of the work. Senior says that the worst thing a mom can be defined as today is not a bad housewife, but a bad mom. You and I aren't housewives anymore; instead we are stay-at-home *moms*. This change reflects that the "pressures on women have gone from keeping an immaculate *house* to being an irreproachable mom."[2]

Senior goes on to say:

> Back in the fifties, women were told to master the differences between oven cleaners and floor wax and special sprays for wood; today they're told to master the differences between toys that hone problem-solving skills and those that encourage imaginative play. This subtle shift in language suggests that playing with one's child is not really play but a job, just as keeping house once was.[3]

What I want us to see as we examine the role that children play in our work is that the different manifestations of our work are not in competition with each other. They go together. You cannot separate the laundry from the children who wear the clean clothes. But what I also want us to see is that the home comprises not just children, but spouses, and sometimes other relatives. I want us to have a more robust view of how our work impacts the people who walk through the doors of our homes. We are all contributors and recipients of the good work done here. The home is about the people in our home. They are our neighbors.

Your Neighbor Is Closer Than You Think

When I was in college, I wanted to be a missionary. While that life is still not out of the question for us, I had a misplaced understanding of what it meant to be radical in my love for my neighbor and those who don't know Christ. I would cry when I read testimonies of missionaries who died on the mission field or made great personal sacrifices for the sake of people who didn't know Christ. Sacrifice for the lost was big on my priority list. Loving my neighbor meant going someplace far away and giving my life for those people. These days I'm in a different context. I don't live in a faraway place (unless you count living in the southern United States as living far away). My life is not in constant danger. I live in the suburbs, in a house with running water, and my fridge is stocked with food. Like many, I regularly ask myself: *Am I loving my neighbor? Am I doing something for Christ's kingdom?*

Our Christian subculture emphasizes loving our neighbor, which is good, but we often forget that we have neighbors living in close proximity to us. If our at-home work is a way we love God by loving others, then we love God by loving the other people *under our roof* whom God has given us. On any given day, you come in contact with multiple "neighbors." If you are married, your husband is your neighbor. If you have children, your children are your neighbors. If you live on a street lined with houses or in an apartment building, the people who live next to you are your neighbors. Your grocer is your neighbor. Your mail carrier is your neighbor. Proximity may change, but everyone you come in contact with is your neighbor.

Martin Luther is known for saying that if our work is not done for the good of our neighbor, then it is of no real value.[4] Your work cannot be done for your own glory, to solicit the praise of others, or to find purpose in your life. It must be done with your neighbor in view. Your work at home is actually a God-given opportunity to serve your neighbor with your good works. It is an opportunity to love others in Jesus's name. It is a chance for you to put aside your comfort for the benefit of another.

In Luke 10:25–37, Jesus answers a lawyer's question, "Who is my neighbor?" with a parable. You are probably familiar with the parable of the good Samaritan. Earlier, the lawyer had asked how he could gain eternal life. Jesus affirmed the lawyer when he answered that he must love God with all his heart, soul, strength, and mind and also his neighbor as himself. This brought up the neighbor question.

Jesus, knowing the lawyer's heart's intentions, turns the conversation back to him. Asking about his neighbor is the wrong question. This is why Jesus uses the Samaritan's mercy to highlight neighborly love. Everyone is our neighbor. Mercy to all is better than mercy to some. The fact that the lawyer was asking who his neighbor was in the first place reveals a heart that truly doesn't comprehend the law or God's grace. He was quick to jump at the chance to obey the law (which he saw as a bunch of rules to follow), but Jesus shows the lawyer (and us) that his neighbor (and ours) is closer than we think, and loving our neighbor is actually showing our love for God.

Like the young lawyer, when confronted with Jesus's command to love our neighbor, we find ourselves asking the question, "And who is my neighbor?" when our neighbor is standing right in front of us asking for a snack. It is popular to love our neighbors outside of our homes, whether it is through community involvement, local church ministry, or overseas missions. We are all part of the movement to do something radical for the least of these in our midst. Of course, there is a time and place for loving the neighbors outside of the home. But the people in your home are recipients of your work too. And just because these people happen to reside inside your home does not mean they are any less significant. The work of the home is as much about the relationships you have with the people of the home as it is about the tasks of the home. The people who eat the food you prepare matter. The people who wear the ironed shirts matter. The people who walk on the swept floors, bathe in the clean bathtub, and finish a craft on a clean desk matter. Work, as I've been saying, is an opportunity to love God through loving others. My friend Miriam often says that she views her work at home as a tangible opportunity to obey Jesus's command to love the "least of these" (Matt. 25:40). Her children can give her nothing in return, but she can still serve and love them.

Luther spent a lot of time explaining how the work we do is the God-ordained way we love our neighbors. You may know Luther for shattering the idea that our salvation can be earned and for emphasizing that salvation rests solely on God's grace. But his understanding of work is actually closely tied to his understanding of salvation:

> If you find yourself in a work by which you accomplish something good for God, or the holy, or yourself, but not for your neighbor alone, then you should know that that work is not a good work. For each one ought to live, speak, act, hear, suffer, and die in love and service for another, even for one's enemies, a husband for his wife and children, a wife for her husband, children for their parents, servants for their masters, masters for their servants, rulers for their subjects and subjects for their rulers, so that one's hand, mouth, eye, foot, heart and desire is for others; these are Christian works, good in nature.[5]

Our good works go forth horizontally (toward our neighbor), while our faith alone (not a result of works) is directed heavenward. We can love our neighbor and serve him or her through our work *because* we have been transformed by grace alone, through faith alone.

Understanding this truth can transform how and why we work. Work is not for us. It is not for our own fulfillment. It is not for our own glorification or status in the world. It is for our neighbor. "All stations are so oriented that they serve others," Luther says.[6] Most of us instinctively know that the work of the home is serving the people of the home simply by the very nature of it. But do you grasp how vital this is? Do you see that by serving the people of your home, by building relationships with them, you are participating in God's cosmic plan to love his creation through your efforts? This turns the cultural tension of children being the focal point of the home on its head. We can't separate the two from each other. Laundry is for *people* to wear. Food is for *people* to be nourished. Clean floors are for *people* to crawl around on. Dishes are for *people* to eat off. The people and the physical work of the home are not in competition. They are two sides of the same coin. Sometimes one aspect of the work gets more attention than the other, but they go together. The physical work of the home exists for the physical people in the home. Let's look at those people.

You Serve Me, I Serve You

My husband was scrolling through Facebook recently when he came across this status update from a friend: "When your hubby asks if you want to clean and organize the garage on his day off! #ilovetoclean #organizingisfun #hegetsme."

We talked about how her husband's personal preference might not have been to clean the garage on his day off, but he chose to love his wife by doing something she enjoyed— which was cleaning and organizing the garage. He displayed love for his neighbor (his wife) through this project, and in turn he showed his love for the God who created her.

Your spouse is the direct recipient of your work in the home. If you are the primary caregiver at home, then you have an opportunity every day to think of ways to honor and work for the husband God has given you. But the primary wage earner can also contribute to the work of the home through even the most ordinary tasks, like organizing the garage.

If you struggle to see how both spouses are contributors to the work of the home, let Martin Luther encourage you:

> Now observe that when that clever harlot, our natural reason (which the pagans followed in trying to be most clever), takes a look at married life, she turns up her nose and says, "Alas, must I rock the baby, wash its diapers, make its bed, smell its stench, stay up nights with it, take care of it when it cries, heal its rashes and sores, and on top of that care for my wife, provide for her, labour at my trade, take care of this and take care of that, do this and do that, endure this and endure that, and whatever else of bitterness and drudgery married life involves? What, should I make such a prisoner of myself? You poor, wretched fellow, have you taken a wife? Fie, fie upon such wretchedness and bitterness! It is better to remain free and lead a peaceful, carefree life; I will become a priest or a nun and compel my children to do likewise."
>
> What then does Christian faith say to this? It opens its eyes, looks upon all these insignificant, distasteful, and despised duties in the Spirit, and is aware that they are all adorned with divine approval as with the costliest gold and jewels. It says, "God, because I am certain that thou hast created me as a man and hast from my body begotten this child, I also know for a certainty that it meets with thy perfect pleasure. I confess to thee that I am not worthy to rock

the little babe or wash its diapers, or to be entrusted with the care of the child and its mother. How is it that I, without any merit, have come to this distinction of being certain that I am serving thy creature and thy most precious will? How gladly will I do so, though the duties should be even more insignificant and despised. Neither frost nor heat, neither drudgery nor labour, will distress or dissuade me, for I am certain that it is thus pleasing in thy sight."

A wife too should regard her duties in the same light, as she suckles the child, rocks and bathes it, and cares for it in other ways; and as she busies herself with other duties and renders help and obedience to her husband. These are truly golden and noble works.[7]

Not much has changed in five hundred years, has it? But this idea that we are contributors to the work of the home is not new. It's been around since even Luther's day.

My husband travels a fair amount for his job, which means a lot of the work at home falls to me. He contributes to the work of the home when he is in town, but some weeks he isn't even in the same state as us, let alone the same house. He also feels loved by a clean house. So when I know he is almost home, I try to make sure the house is in order (as much as possible!) so he doesn't walk into chaos. He can think more clearly and even serve us in his contribution to the home if he comes home to an orderly atmosphere. We each are recipients of the work of the home, and we each are contributors. We love each other, our neighbors, through our work.

What about the Children?

We've already seen how children are our neighbors and how they are recipients of our work. They might be smaller and less mature than we are, but they are still our neighbors. Let's look at how they are also contributors to the work of the home.

Much has been written about the current state of childhood in America. And because my children are so young, I won't pretend to understand what it takes to raise kids who contribute to the work of the home, or even broader society. But I do know that part of our work is establishing the foundation that the home we all live in is for us all, and therefore requires that we *all* contribute to it. So to help think through this more clearly, I've enlisted the help of some friends.

My sister-in-law has a saying she tells her children (ages six, four, and one): "This home is for everyone." When her six-year-old leaves his dinosaurs all over the floor, making the floor impassable for others or leaving them in a place where his little brother may find them and try to eat them, she reminds him that he is a contributor to the home and needs to be responsible for his toys. The home is his place too. This directly applies Luther's understanding that our vocation is lived in community. In Luther's view a vocation couldn't honor God if the man or woman lived a cloistered life (like a monk) because vocation is for one's neighbor, not to give good works back to God. So, cleaning up his toys is for the good of his family. It's so his brother does not choke on small pieces. It's so his parents don't trip on what they can't see. And it's so his sister also has room to play with her toys. He is a contributor to the work of the home by simply obeying his mom's request to clean up his toys when he is finished playing with them.

In a series of parenting seminars, Jeff and Jen Wilkin discuss how they trained their children to see their chores as a vital component to sustaining their family. Their children were responsible for keeping their rooms clean and for other specific chores. In their neighborhood, many families chose to have a lawn service take care of their yard work. The Wilkins chose to teach their children how to mow the grass rather than pay for a service to do it. Wanting their children to understand the value of work as contribution, they taught their children how to work together and to work as contributors to the family home. When Jen took a part-time job, the children's contribution to the work of the home became even more vital to keeping everything running.[8]

Keeping up with the housework has been a struggle for me ever since I learned how to dress myself and throw my dirty clothes in a pile on the floor. (Ask my parents!) On more than one occasion, I was on the receiving end of an exhortation to value my things and the home I lived in. As a member of the family, I was in a community of people. My brothers and parents were my neighbors. Loving them meant picking up my clothes off the floor, putting my dirty dish in the dishwasher, and learning how to clean the bathrooms. And while loving our children through our work and teaching them how to be enthusiastic contributors is part of the purpose for our work, all that we do is moving us (and them) toward something beyond the walls of our home.

When the Roles Are Reversed

The people who are in our home are not always our children or spouses. Often others come under our care. An aging parent needs more hands-on attention. A sick relative needs a place to live. Grandchildren need primary caregivers who are stable or not working full time. The work of the home affects a lot of people, but for the one who is already at home, this care often falls on her.

My mom experienced this firsthand when she first cared

for my grandma before she died and then my grandpa in his final months. My grandpa was in congestive heart failure, so he needed someone to take him to doctors' appointments and keep up with his medicine. Toward the end, he needed a place to live because he no longer could live on his own. My mom did all of that for him. She compared it to having a child again, yet without the youthful energy that accompanies young parents and with the added awkwardness of it being your parent, not the child you birthed. The roles were suddenly reversed, and she wasn't watching her child grow before her eyes; she was watching her dad waste away until he drew his final breath.

Isn't this a beautiful picture of loving your neighbor? In the parable of the good Samaritan, the man who had been beaten by robbers could do nothing to repay the Samaritan's gift of kindness toward him. The man was beaten and helpless, and the Samaritan cared for him anyway. This was my mom, and this is all those who care for aging relatives who can do nothing in return. This is the cycle of care that we all face. Likely most of us will at some point be required to give this kind of care, and most of us will one day find ourselves needing this kind of care. When the roles are reversed, we are still loving our neighbor.

Eyes to See God

As you love your people through your work, you also give them a vision for something greater. As God's image bearer, you point to a deeper spiritual reality that gives those under your care a category for seeing God. Your nearest neighbors see that God is with them through your hands-on care for them.

Michael Horton says:

> Just as we wouldn't expect to find the Creator of the universe in a feeding trough of a barn in some obscure village,

much less hanging bloody, on a Roman cross, we do not expect to find him delivering his extraordinary gifts in such human places and in such humble ways as human speech, a bath, and a meal. This can't be right, we reason. We need signs and wonders to know God is with us. Yet it is only because God has promised to meet us in the humble and ordinary places, to deliver his inheritance, that we are content to receive him in these ways.[9]

As we saw in the previous chapter, the work you do is not meaningless. This is true not only because you participate in bringing order out of chaos, but also because as you work in the mundane, the ordinary, you help the people in your home see that God, the provider and sustainer of all things, is with them. Kathleen Norris says that "the child who is thus fed by a mother's love eventually learns to trust in others, and also in God."[10] We are the vehicles by which our neighbors see the God who created them.

As you feed hungry bellies, you are pointing to a God who makes sure even the sparrows get their food (Matt. 6:26–27). As you attend parent/teacher conferences, dress a sick relative, or buy new clothes for growing kids, you are pointing to a God who cares so much for his creation that he even clothes the lilies of the field (Matt. 6:28–30). Every meal made with love, every fork that has been cleaned to protect against spreading illness, every toilet wiped clean helps shift your family's gaze toward the God who keeps everything together and is making all things new (Rev. 21:5). With your work you are telling your family that we serve a God who is present, who is among us.

In his book *Luther on Vocation*, Gustaf Wingren summarizes Martin Luther by saying: "God's complete work is set in motion through vocation: he changes the world and he sheds his mercy on hard-pressed humanity. . . . Through vocation God's presence is really with man."[11]

And there is no greater way to love your neighbors than to remind them of this astounding truth—God is with us.

Our culture tells us that children are ultimate, that they are our identity and focus. As the work of the home has taken a backseat to the people in the home (*stay-at-home mom* versus *housewife*), we need to grasp the idea that the work of the home is for the people in the home, yes, but that they are also participants in the home, contributors to the home. While the physical work of the home may fall apart, the children and their legacy will last forever. We need to recover the idea that the home is for everyone—our children, our spouses, and anyone else God brings under our care. There can be no separating the physical work of the home from the people in it because both depend on each other. Children need to view the work happening in the home as an important contribution and that it serves the neighbors among us. Actually, we all need to understand this truth. It propels us forward to the communities that we live in. In addition to our work being for the people inside, we are not lone rangers. We don't work and exist in isolation. Despite the American notion that we are autonomous individuals who don't need anyone else, how we work and how we feel in our work tells us otherwise. And that is where we are headed in the next chapter.

Getting Practical

Callie is one of nine children. Growing up in a home with that many children required a fair amount of coordinating. Callie's mom, Amber, created a system for how the chores would get done. Every child was assigned a chore for the year based on his or her age, and when you got older you graduated to a different chore. In many ways, the new chore was a sign of greater responsibility in the family; as you grew older, you got a chore that required more thought and care. But it was also a sign of your contribution to the family. If everyone did not contribute to the work of the home, then the home would fall apart. They all needed each other in order to thrive, to eat, to have clean clothes, to have mown grass, and the list could go on. This spirit of contribution has followed Callie into adulthood in two ways. She is often the first to see a need and the first to meet that need. She sees herself as a contributor to the lives of others in the same way she was a contributor to her home growing up. But she is also passing on the legacy of contribution to her own children in her home. Before he could utter a complete sentence, her oldest son learned how to help unload the dishwasher. Now he is able to unload the silverware into the drawers. His part as a contributor is being instilled in him at a young age in part because of the legacy of his grandmother, who taught her children to be contributors to the work of the home.

What are some ways you can encourage your children to be contributors to the work of the home? Do you feel the tension between the work of the home and the people of the home? How do you resolve this tension?

5

It Takes a Village

When my twins first started at Mother's Day Out, I was afraid to tell people. For three years they had been at home with me every day, and this was the first time I was sending them somewhere. I was sad. I missed them. I felt a little guilty for leaving them. But more than anything I felt shame. I felt like a failure. Walking them through those doors to their classroom felt like a commentary on what I was able, or not able, to do in a given day. And if I'm honest, it was absolutely true. You see, I put them in Mother's Day Out because I really needed the break in the morning. We don't live near family. My husband travels fairly regularly for his job. Most of our church friends are also in the same boat as us—trying to navigate life with very small children. Putting them in Mother's Day Out was my white flag. It was my acknowledgment that I really could not do it all, no matter how much I tried. The work of the home is not a job for one person, no matter how hard we try to make it one. It really is a community effort.

Shonda Rimes, television producer and mother of three, recently explained why she felt compelled to talk about her nanny in her book:

> I think a lot of successful women don't talk about the fact that they have help because it feels shameful. I mean we are all supposed to be doing this all ourselves, which is crazy, because we work. If you're working, how else are you doing it? You are not a magic person. You can't split yourself in two. You're not Hermione Granger with a Time-Turner. You have to have somebody help you. And there's no shame in that.[1]

Rimes is getting at a common theme of at-home work. We are proud to go it alone. Her point is that we aren't able to do all that is required of us. But, boy, do we like to try. In our Christian world of at-home work, we might look at a woman like Rimes and say, "Of course she needs help; she has a full-time job outside of the home." What if the stay-at-home mom hires a cleaning crew to clean her house once a month? What if the children go to Mother's Day Out? What if the dad watches the kids while the mom goes to lunch with friends, runs to the grocery store, or just needs a moment to unwind? What if everyone in the home is part of the spring cleaning your house desperately needs? Is this a failure in our work? Or are we, like Rimes, in need of a team of people to help us in our work?

Two key terms define how humans work: *community* and *collaboration*. Community is the network of people you work alongside who share the workload. If you worked in an office setting, community would be your coworkers who cover for you in a meeting when you are sick, who pick up your printed papers at the copier, or who work with you on a big presentation. Collaboration occurs when you use that network of people to make you better in your work. When you don't understand what your boss is asking you to do, you have coworkers to give you clarity. When you are stuck on an idea, you can brainstorm with a team of people. Community and collaboration are essential (and often missing) in our work at home.

In bygone days, children would learn the trade of their parents. This required children to be in close proximity not only to their parents, but also to a network of people who loved them and cared about their growth in their trade. This applied to at-home work too. In fact, for a long time (as we saw in chap. 1), the work of the home was a family endeavor.

A couple of summers ago my husband and I wanted to re-purpose a dresser into a television stand for our living room. We were planning to do it eventually, but when my parents came to visit, my dad offered to help Daniel with the project. My dad has lived longer than us, owned more homes than us, and knows more about a variety of household projects. He showed Daniel what tools he needed, purchased the tools, and helped him strip, sand, and paint our new television stand. He also showed him how to install a ceiling fan and powerwash our house. Often when a house project comes up, Daniel will comment that it would be nice to live near people like my dad, who are eager to pass on their knowledge and know more than us about all that is involved with home ownership.

We no longer live in a cultural context where men take on the family business and stay close to home. Jobs take us far away from friends and family, from community. Additionally, when the majority of people in our neighborhoods work outside of the home, gone for ten to twelve hours a day, many of us don't have a neighbor to call when we need someone to meet our child at the bus stop. So what can you do in light of all these changes? You can't just reminisce about 1950s' housewives or 1800s' family units and call them a win for at-home work. Nostalgia never saved anyone. And as tempting as it may be to just adopt another culture's ideas, we have to apply the theology of work to our cultural context. We may never live in a close-knit community where everyone has a share of the at-home work, but we can learn from those who have gone before us and try to shift the path away from isolation to a more robust community effort.

Community and Culture

Throughout history, the work of the home has been done in the context of community. Gloria Furman, wife, mother of four, and author, lives in a community-oriented culture. She wrote to me that it is actually the norm for at-home work to be done in the context of community.

> If you look at a population density map, it's fun to envision how the majority of people in the world are community-oriented. That is, being embedded in a community/family is the lens through which they see themselves and others. Therefore, when they see me doing things by myself (housework, taking kids to the pediatrician, grocery shopping, walking somewhere, sitting in a queue, etc.), they see my alone-ness and "feel sorry" for me, asking the questions, "Where is your nanny today?" "Why don't you have a helper?" In their view of our work, being a mother is too much work for one woman.

But in Western culture, this is hardly the case. At-home work rarely (if ever) happens within a larger community. For the most part, if you live in Western society, you are going it alone. With the exception of those who live near family or are involved in a local church with a lot of stay-at-home moms, finding community, or a place where you can share the burden of the work with others, for the stay-at-home mom requires a good degree of intentionality. It's not a given anymore.

Some are seeking to change that. *The New York Times* reported on a growing number of urban families who are staying in the city after they have children instead of retreating to the suburbs because of the relationships they have built in their buildings and neighborhoods.

> "As the kids have come together, so have the parents," said Mr. Goepfert, whose daughter is 2. "We have dinners together, share toys, hand-me-downs, get help with last-minute babysitting. That kind of community isn't all that common in New York, and it fosters an environment that's so valuable that we turned down a significant amount of money."[2]

What this family, and others, captures is a deeply engrained need for community that makes up our personhood. Within your at-home work, you can see this need in a variety of ways. As you understand that your work is ultimately for the benefit of your neighbor, then work becomes something done not in isolation, but within a larger community of people. It's done for people, and it's done with people.

Collaboration

Collaboration is another component to at-home work that gets lost in how we go about our work. Collaboration is the bringing together of minds to understand a common idea. Historically, the work of the home was largely done in the context of community. When a mother had a question about her child's fever, she had a network of flesh-and-blood mothers (old and young) to tap into. There were remedies for childhood illnesses buried in the brains of seasoned mothers who had gone before her. When you made too much dinner, you had a community to share it with. When your rolls didn't rise like they were supposed to, you could sit with another woman while she made her rolls that always seemed to rise perfectly. You had someone to help you with child care. Even the process of having babies involved midwives who were usually your mother, sisters, or aunts. Within the context of a larger community, everyone was a collaborator.

In our work at home, community and collaboration go together. Collaboration is part of what makes work successful. In one sense, we crave community because we need collaboration. We need the relationships people provide us and the ideas they can give us. Proverbs 15:22 says that "without counsel plans fail." The best businesses are the ones where everyone works together. Good homes work together too.

In the absence of real-life people to collaborate with, we now turn to our most trusted resource and tool in our work—the Internet. Collaboration and community is so important to stay-at-home moms that an entire industry has been built around women writing strictly about the mom life. They are called the "mommy bloggers." As of this writing, 14 percent of all mothers are "mommy bloggers." There are 3.9 million "mommy blogs," and about five hundred of them have considerable reach.[3] These blogs offer everything from how to homeschool to how to get stains out of your carpet. Collaboration is happening in at-home work; it's just happening in new and unconventional ways. When you don't have a community of people to call on for collaboration, the "mommy bloggers" and online forums provide a needed outlet. Who hasn't Googled a symptom at three o'clock in the morning rather than call your mom? Who hasn't built an entire recipe library from Pinterest or watched a YouTube tutorial on how to fold a fitted sheet? This form of collaboration through the Internet isn't the problem, but it perpetuates the isolation that our work affords us. It's a lot easier to type a question into your smartphone than it is to pick up the telephone and call someone for help. But if work is ultimately about relationships, then sometimes that might be the necessary solution to remind yourself that no one is an island—mom included.

While I can argue all day long that community and collaboration are vital to at-home work, you may not fully grasp the need for them (or make the necessary changes) until you understand why they are important to begin with.

It Is Not Good to Be Alone

You and I were not meant to be alone. We were not meant to work alone. God created us in relationship with him and in relationship to others. To be human has always been to be in community with other human beings. Adam and Eve existed together. In fact, one of God's first declarations about Adam was that it was not good for him to be alone (Gen. 2:18). To be an image bearer is to live in community with other image bearers because the One we image (God) eternally lives in community with himself (the Trinity). From the beginning of time, God has been making a people for himself, to live in relationship with him and relationship with one another. Our lives were never intended to be lived alone. And if work is about loving God by loving others, community and collaboration are essential components of our work. The current model of at-home work in our culture (suburban or urban mom working alone with the kids all day) perpetuates feelings of loneliness that characterize many stay-at-home moms.

Gene Edward Veith says that part of what it means to be

human is to build and develop society. Work, our vocation, is done for people and with people.

> From the beginning, God put us in families, tribes, societies. God ordained that we be in relationships. He ordained that we need each other. From ancient hunters and gatherers who had to join together to bring down a buffalo that is much stronger than any one of them, to the complex division of labor in modern industrial economies, we are all in this together.
>
> But if it is true that we are supposed to be dependent on other people, it is also true that other people are supposed to be dependent on us. This [is] an active exchange; my gifts for yours; my vocation for your vocation.[4]

This is community and collaboration at its best. Communities exist and work with and for each other, and every vocation is used and appreciated. This is how God created you to operate with others.

In a blog post talking about the first few months after her twins were born, counselor and author Heather Davis Nelson recounts how it truly took a community of people to help her get on her feet and care for her twin babies.

> God gave us much, much more than we could handle by giving us twins, precisely so that we would begin to learn to lean on the help that was surrounding us—that we'd learn to live in the "village" in which God placed us.
>
> A crucial part of being part of a vibrant village-like community is *the ability to ask for and receive help*, not only the ability to give help.[5]

I can relate to this. When my twin boys were born eight weeks early, I was not prepared for their arrival, let alone what it took to care for premature babies in the NICU. Because I had a cesarean section, I was not able to drive to visit them unless my husband wasn't working. So for five weeks, our church provided rides for me to the hospital every morning (with a lunchtime pick-up). They provided meals for us so I could rest when I wasn't at the hospital. They were our village when we could not care for our tiny babies alone. And who were the ones who primarily gave me rides? Women who stayed home. Without their support, I would never have been able to get to the hospital to hold my babies. I wouldn't have been able to bring them pumped milk every morning. I needed the community, and the community stepped up in support. This time of life solidified for me the truth of the saying "it takes a village to raise a child."

Others have reflected on what is gained by seeing at-home work as a community effort. Author Hannah Anderson says this about the need for community:

> God did not intend for families to be islands; they are part of the continent. This is why multi-generational communities are so important to the work of home. It's not simply about older women giving younger women advice or household tips. It's about women (and men) in a completely different season of life being able to step in and say, "Here, let me hold the baby while you take a shower." Another mommy friend might offer to do this for me, but she probably hasn't showered for several days herself. Today, we're in a place where we're building stronger ties with community. It's not unusual for me to get a last minute text from a friend asking me to pick up her kids from school; or for me to send one asking her to do the same. Now that my children are older, working in Sunday School or the nursery doesn't drain me

the way they used to. I enjoy being the one to hold the babies and give younger moms a break.[6]

We also see this desire for community and collaboration in the variety of playgroups, Bible studies, gym classes, and MOPS groups that exist all over our cities offering women a network of other women in their same season of life. These groups understand the desire and need for community that arise in a woman the minute she brings the baby home from the hospital and realizes that it is just her and the baby all day long. After she became a mom, one woman I talked to told me she enrolled her daughter in a swimming class as one way to meet other parents. Because she already had a network of people to draw from, the class wasn't her sole source of community. But for some parents in the class it was. She felt their needs acutely as she got to know other parents who were in similar life stages. Community mattered, and many didn't know where to find it, so they grasped for it in the form of an infant swim class. Many look for it wherever they can get it—at the park, the library, PTA—anywhere they can find other parents engaged in the same work as them. But Christians have a better answer to this longing for community and collaboration.

The Local Church and the At-Home Mom

There is a reason that the Bible often uses the language of the family when talking about the people of God. We have been adopted into his family through Christ (Eph. 1:5). We are awaiting a future home with him (Eph. 2:19; Phil. 3:20). The home here on earth is a microcosm of the heavenly reality that awaits us. But so is the church. Our individual families are pointing toward the family of God. So while not everyone has a mom who can come help her when her baby is born, or a dad who can show her how to use power tools, the church is full of mothers and fathers who can provide this community and collaboration, but also take it to the next level.

We hear a lot about Titus 2 and how it applies to ministering to women, often in the context of a discipleship relationship between older women and younger women. This is good and right. But this passage of Scripture is also about living in community with another.

> But as for you, teach what accords with sound doctrine. Older men are to be sober-minded, dignified, self-controlled, sound in faith, in love, and in steadfastness. Older women likewise are to be reverent in behavior, not slanderers or slaves to much wine. They are to teach what is good, and so train the young women to love their husbands and children, to be self-controlled, pure, working at home, kind, and submissive to their own husbands, that the word of God may not be reviled. (Titus 2:1–5)

Paul tells Titus that the older women are to teach good things to the younger women, so that God's Word is honored among them. Included in the list of good things is how to love the people in our homes. God's Word is honored in your work at home. Women who have lived longer know a thing or two about how to love our nearest neighbors. They have something that younger women don't have—perspective, which is vital to the mom who can't see beyond the dirty countertops, the fussy baby, or the rebellious teenager. They continue the chain of help and discipleship that was done for them years before, and they do it all within the context of a local body of believers who gather together to worship Christ and to spread his name to a watching world. Community done among women commends the gospel to a world that breathes isolation and autonomy. I like to call it "Christ-shaped community in the home." This is taking your heart craving of community in your work and connecting you with mentors and teachers who have walked your path before.

But this Christ-shaped community is not just about getting more help in your work. It's pointing you toward the purpose of your work. When you gather for worship, you gather with your true family. When you work alongside them in your work, you are putting feet on the preached Word. The early church knew this well. They gathered in homes for their worship gatherings (Acts 16:13–15, 40). They met the needs of the apostles and fellow Christians (2 Cor. 9:11–13). They bonded together over suffering and plundering of their property (Heb. 10:34). They knew what all of their work was pointing toward—our future home.

While groups outside of the church are helpful and have their place, it is only within the local church that you will be given a vision beyond the mundane realties of life and given eyes to see the God who has given you this good work to do for the good of the world.

Later Life

Community and collaboration among women look different based on season of life and the women in each context. The important thing is that we are open to fostering these relationships and that we allow for freedom of personality and gifts. The work of the home is seasonal. Ecclesiastes reminds us that there is a time for everything (3:1–8). There is a time for sleepless nights and warming bottles, and there is a time for discipleship over coffee and taking a meal to a friend in need. It's easy in the years with young children to think that you are doing little to impact your community. Perhaps most weeks you rarely leave your home—you just don't have the capacity to do much else.

Know that there are seasons to at-home work. Some seasons provide more opportunities for community involvement. Some seasons require you to be the one being helped more than you are helping others. But it's only a season. It won't last forever. (Or at least I hear that it won't!)

Seeing your impact within the community of believers as cyclical is so helpful. It ebbs and flows, eventually flowing back to more involvement and more service to others. It just takes time. I am encouraged by the lives of women who have gone before me and are using their later years to love their communities, their churches, and their families.

Cecile Bledsoe, who was at home for many years, is an Arkansas state senator. When I had a conversation with her about her leadership role and what prepared her for it, her insights struck me. "Those years [at home] were not a waste," she says. They were the training ground for her leadership. All of her time spent saving money on groceries, keeping the family's schedules in order, negotiating with people who were fixing things around her home, and getting to know her neighbors prepared her to do similar work on a much larger scale as a state senator. The work at home mattered in the moment, and it prepared her children for the world and prepared her for the leadership work in the Senate.

But at-home work is more than just preparation for something beyond the little years. Often when the children are grown and gone, women struggle to see how the work of the home is still valuable. After all, there is only so much you can clean and cook when there aren't children tracking mud inside or raiding the refrigerator. How does this work have value when the home looks different?

Carol Jenkins is a wife, mother, and grandmother. She has spent a large part of her life serving her community. Even while she had children in her home, her kids remember her as always being ready to take a meal to someone, to volunteer in the community, or to help her neighbors. As I spoke with Carol about how she continues to see her work in the home as valuable now that her children are grown, she remarked that sometimes it is as simple as having loaves of bread in the freezer ready to give to a church member recovering from surgery or adjusting to a new baby. For her, the important thing is being available to meet a need whenever it arises. This highlights the fact that the work of the home matters even after the years of diapers and stained clothes. The work of the home serves the world.

I experience this with my friend, Robin. Robin is the mother of four children who are now grown and out of the house. Now she regularly gives her time to serve me. She watches my boys so I can get out for a bit, sometimes to write and sometimes to simply go to the store with my hands free. One night she watched my kids so my husband and I could attend a Christmas dinner. Before we left, I noticed the laundry had piled up again in my baby's laundry basket, but I didn't have time to start a load. When we returned later that evening, I was surprised to hear the dryer going. Robin had noticed the full basket and did the laundry for me. I nearly cried, especially because laundry is the one task I barely stay on top of. But this is community in action. My friends and I have remarked that Robin is the type of woman we want to be when we are older. We want to embrace a compelling and generous self-giving nature. Whether it's meeting for coffee with a discouraged mother of a teenager or holding a baby so a new mom can take a nap, this type of service gives dignity to at-home work. It reminds the woman in the trenches that her work matters.

These three women embody the cyclical nature of how at-home work thrives in community in any season. They remind us that while we are also shaped and encouraged by our community, our work allows us to shape the community. We all need each other to keep the wheels moving in the work of the home. In some seasons you are shaping your small community (your children), and in others your community-shaping is much broader—holding the quiet corners of society together. And people at every stage are vitally important.

When Community Is Crucial

One aspect of at-home work in particular needs an extra dose of community involvement. Of course, we all need relationships in our work, but for people in nontraditional circumstances, the isolation can be even more crushing. Rachael is a mother of three. Her oldest son has autism, and recently her family became the primary caretakers for her father-in-law (who has Alzheimer's). I talked with Rachael about the role the local church can play in providing community for stay-at-home moms with children who have special needs and/or who provide care for the sick.

> I do feel very isolated in the sense that I can talk with any mom in any gathering and we can talk about relatable parenting things, but there is always that dynamic that is so different. What we are doing in school with Jack is so different than what others are doing. It feels very alone. Who else really understands this? Knowing other parents who are in similar circumstances is helpful, but they usually aren't believers.

When I asked Rachael how the local church plays a role in providing community for parents in her situation, she said that if she wants people to relate to her life, she has outlets for that. But what she needs more than anything is to know how the hope of the gospel applies to her circumstances. Often we think that we can't relate to people in different circumstances from us, but she is learning that people don't have to know the complexities of her story or even be in a similar situation to understand her.

The need for community doesn't find its resolution in another person to commiserate with about the complexities of life. Instead, that need is resolved at the foot of the cross, where we are leveled in our sin and brokenness. There are unique and real challenges for the mom who spends her days at therapy sessions and doctor's appointments versus the mom who has a relatively healthy child. In many ways this specific kind of work is beyond the scope of this book. But I hope we understand that the local church plays a vital role in providing opportunities for everyone (regardless of their season and circumstances) to connect with other believers for their own good and for the witness of the church to a watching world.

In Our Bones

Your desire for collaboration and community in your work is more than just an attempt to get things done or fill an empty void in a lonely soul. It is vital to your thriving as a human being made in the image of God. You were made to be in community, to work with and among others. Titus 2, which embraces the community-building nature of the local church and shows that we are not able to do life all on our own, tells us that only God is sufficient to get all things done well. We weren't made to do this work on our own. We need older and wiser saints to help us. Titus 2 gets that. Community keeps you and me on our knees and humble before the throne of God's grace daily. It encourages us when we are fainthearted in our work. It sustains us when we are weak. And it helps us see that our work is good work.

Getting Practical

Every Christmas we go to my parents' house, so like every December, I was spending the final days before our trip wrapping presents, packing for a family of five, and getting our house in order. Robin had asked me at church the Sunday before if my husband would be able to help me before we left (in two days). Because he was also leaving his work behind, he had far too much to do to wrap up his year before our trip. Before I could even finish telling her what I was planning on doing the next day, which included running errands around town with all three kids in tow, Robin said, "Let me come over tomorrow morning so you can get your errands done." My initial response was, "Thank you! But I think I'll be fine." Thankfully, it was an internal response. What came out was, "Oh, thank you so much. That would be such a help to me." And I needed that help.

The work of the home is too much for one person to handle. In that moment, on that day, I was reminded again that community is crucial in my work. It's not optional. How can you allow for community and collaboration in your work? How can you be that community and collaboration for someone else?

6

Miles to Go before I Sleep

After every vacation, my husband inevitably goes back to work buried in e-mails. Because he is in sales, he always has customers in need of his product, so while he might be off from work on a vacation, his customers are not. In an ever-connected digital age, work never stops. If someone has access to a computer (or smartphone), he has access to work, and it is hard to get away sometimes. My experience after a vacation is a little different. While I may not come home to an inbox full of e-mails, I come home to another monstrosity—laundry. Maybe it's my season of life (three kids under three) or maybe it is just the fact that there are five people in our house, but laundry is my overflowing inbox. Everything else takes a vacation when we are gone (the cleaning, the cooking, etc.), but the laundry just keeps coming. It sleeps for no one.

Whatever part of your work is overflowing when you end your vacation, we all face this dilemma, don't we? Rest or keep working? Sleep or organize last season's clothes? Read a book for fun or spend the afternoon working on the budget? Watch a movie while the kids sleep or rake the leaves?

Robert Frost alludes to this in his famous poem, "Stopping by Woods on a Snowy Evening." Though he's tired, and the dark and quiet woods are inviting, he must keep going because he has things he promised to do. Sleep is calling him, but he knows it is far off.[1]

While many interpret Frost's "sleep" as death, you probably feel the pull of literal sleep every morning when your alarm clock goes off. Or when your child crawls in bed with you. Every day you face reminders that you have miles to go before you can rest.

Parents often lament that sleep is elusive. As I write this, I have spent two consecutive nights up with a sick child. On top of the work that always seems to generate more work, it almost seems like a joke to talk about rest in a book on the work of the home. But we must. You were made for rest. In this chapter we are going to look at our need for rest and ways to diagnose our idleness or idolatry in our work, and cast a vision for the pursuit of rest for the good of us and our neighbors.

To Rest Is Human

It's a common misconception that the need for rest points to flaws in our personhood. I once heard someone say that sleep is for weak people, implying that to sleep is to admit defeat. In our self-sufficient culture, that is the exact opposite of the persona we want to display, isn't it? Personally, when I am confronted with my weakness, limitations, or need for a nap, I am bothered and feel like I don't measure up to my own standards for excellence. It grates on me. A number of years ago someone told me that only God gets his to-do list done. And I'm not God, so I should stop trying to measure up.

This need for rest and reprieve from our work goes back to the beginning of creation, when God created Adam and Eve in his likeness, his image. Work is one of the ways that we bear God's image, but rest is another. After God worked to bring forth creation, he rested (Gen. 2:3). As humans living in a fallen world, we don't get the full benefit of enjoyment that God had at creation because we are finite and imperfect. Our work is never complete and it is never perfect. Rest is a God-designed gift meant to point us back to the One who created us and sustains our weary hands in our labors. Sleep is actually his gift to us (Ps. 127:2). If the God of the universe, who wants for nothing, rested, then we his image bearers, who are in want of everything, need rest.

The fact that the command to rest was instituted at creation tells us that rest is not a result of sin. Rest existed before sin entered the world. Like the problems we face in work, the problems we face with rest are a result of sin. The need for rest is not the problem. Rest affords enjoyment of what our hands have made. It's hard to see the work of your hands when your hands are constantly moving. Rest gives opportunities to delight in God's good gifts. It's the whole "stop and smell the roses" idea.

But the command to rest isn't found only in the creation account. Throughout the Old Testament Law, God reminded his people that he was the One who would sustain them and provide for them. God's people had laws about Sabbath rest, laws about Sabbath years, and laws about what could be done on the Sabbath, all designed to point them to the giver of all good things, the God who established the work of their hands (Ex. 20:8–11; 23:11–19; Leviticus 23; 25). In the new covenant, while the law is fulfilled in Christ, we are still reminded of our utter dependence on the Creator for all things. There is nothing that we can do apart from him. Jesus is Lord of the Sabbath (Matt. 12:8), and as the Lord he is our true and complete rest (Heb. 4:9–10). He made the Sabbath for us so we would learn our dependence and finiteness. By trusting in him, we acknowledge that we cannot do everything on our to-do list, and we can do nothing to earn our own salvation. Only he is sufficient for all these things.

Before I move on, I want to acknowledge that there is disagreement among Christians over what observing the Sabbath means for us in the new covenant. I take the position that the Sabbath requirements of the Old Testament were fulfilled in Christ, which means that we are not bound to observe the actual Sabbath day in the way Old Testament Israel did. However, many Christians believe the Bible teaches otherwise. But when I speak of the Sabbath, I speak from my own position on it—that the Sabbath requirement was fulfilled in Christ, and he is now our true rest. As human beings we still have a need for rest, but we are no longer morally obligated to observe the Sabbath in the same way.

J. I. Packer says:

> We need to be aware of our limitations and to let this awareness work in us humility and self-distrust, and a realization of our helplessness on our own. Thus we may learn our need to depend on Christ, our Savior and Lord, at every turn of the road, to practice that dependence as one of the constant habits of our heart, and hereby to discover what Paul discovered before us: "when I am weak, then I am strong" (2 Cor. 12:10).[2]

To acknowledge this helplessness is to fall in line with our position as image bearers. We bear God's image, but we are not God. We are creatures in need of rest and recovery. We are limited in what we can accomplish so that in our weakness we are driven to the God who can accomplish all things. But we also rest because we were made for it. We were made to cease from our labors for the purpose of enjoying the work of our hands.

The reality is that even though our design as image bearers means we need rest, the sweeping effects of sin on every area of our lives means we don't do this well.

Even Our Rest Is Fallen

Because of sin, all work exhausts us on some level. As we saw in chapter 2, work is not the fulfilling, productive, invigorating endeavor God originally designed it to be. Part of the thorns and thistles of our work is exhaustion. At-home work is not immune to this. We feel the need for rest even more deeply than we ever would have in a pre–Genesis 3 world. We were created as limited beings, and sin makes it ever more real and devastating.

In their book *The Gospel at Work*, Greg Gilbert and Sebastian Traeger explore the two primary challenges we face in our work: idolatry and idleness. In their estimation, sin manifests itself into these two primary categories. Both, they say, are celebrated in our society: "We tend to praise those who make work the center of their lives, as well as those who have somehow pushed it out of their lives entirely."[3]

The idol of at-home work is hard to diagnose sometimes. Because you have no boss, no coworkers, and, if you choose, no one else observing how you work, it is easy to get lost in the productivity of the home without ever having the chance to see how your work has consumed you. It is also hard to diagnose because in some Christian subcultures we have made the work of the home the gold standard of womanhood. If a woman is homeschooling her children well, mowing her grass every two weeks, baking bread for her neighbor, and maintaining an immaculate home, we marvel at her labor and say, "I don't know she does it." We send a subtle message that her hard work is a feat to beat. Now, I'm not saying that a woman who does those things has made at-home work an idol. God has given everyone varying capacities and gifts. Some can accomplish more than others. But at the end of the day we need to be able to diagnose idolatry in our own lives, regardless of our capacity. One key way is to check our response to the work that isn't complete. When the laundry doesn't get done, does it ruin your day? When your children misbehave in public, are you distraught about what others might think about your parenting? When you can't make a meal from scratch for your sick friend and instead have to settle on takeout, do you feel like a failure? Does your chest swell with pride when people wonder at your abilities? Perhaps the work of the home has become an idol in your life.

Tim Keller says this about idolatry in our work: "If you make any work the purpose of your life—even if that work is church ministry—you create an idol that rivals God."[4] This can be said of at-home work, too. In our Christian subculture, at-home work is praised as good and faithful work, and I'm thankful for that. But if you find your hope and identity in folded laundry, a spotless refrigerator, and children who praise you from the rooftops, you have misplaced affections regarding your work.

This is hard, I know. For a large part of my working life I have struggled with idleness in work, not idolatry. Or at least that's what I thought. I spent my twenties doing the bare minimum in jobs I hated, while holding out for the weekend when I would be able to do what I wanted. Free time meant lounging on the couch while watching movies. I rarely thought about extra projects or productivity. Something happened to me after I had my children. In some ways, I think God convicted me of my laziness regarding work. But I've swung that pendulum too far at times. When my children don't nap as long as I want them to, and I'm forced to table a writing project or cleaning project for another time, I get angry. When my children don't meet an internal standard I have set for behavior and I'm humiliated in public, I get frustrated. When my to-do list is left undone at the end of another day, I take it out on everyone in my home. This hit me square in the face when I began noticing that I would not take a Sabbath rest on Sunday. Because my husband was home from work, I took that as more time for me to work on things I wanted to work on. He could help with the kids and I could check more things off my to-do list. One morning while listening to a message by D. A. Carson on the book of Nehemiah, I was humbled by my idolatry over my work. He said: "If you can make a little extra money on the Sabbath then why rest on the Sabbath?"[5] I can rephrase that as, if you can knock a few things off the to-do list, then why rest on the Sabbath? I was directly ignoring God's faithful provision for me as a finite being because I valued my to-do list over his Word. I was trying to be Lord over my own life. I was ignoring the fact that as a worshiper of God I am created not just to worship him through my work but also through my rest.

Thankfully, the Lord has convicted me about this idol, but because of my former tendency toward laziness it has been an adjustment for me to adapt and compromise. Work has become an idol in my life, which surprises and grieves me.

Maybe you respond differently when work becomes an idol. Here are some other common manifestations of idolatry in the work of the home.

The Myth of the Supermom

We've all heard of her. We marvel at her and want to be her. Her name is Supermom, and she can get a million things done while also staying healthy and happy. She never needs help. She does it all. And we are left in her perfect wake wondering why we can't accomplish more in our day. We hear a lot about women "having it all" in professional circles, but we struggle with this same temptation in the home too. In some ways, we are tempted to overwork because we want to justify our existence in the world. We don't want to be deemed useless or lazy, so we work harder. Or we think we can do it the best, so we never let anyone else in the home try. All of this is pride. We want others to think well of us, so we work ourselves to death. And in the end no one benefits.

We can also shun help. Instead of seeing the home as a community effort (as we saw in chap. 5), we see the home as a place for us to be the hero of the day. What I was confronted with in my idolatry of at-home work is that I wanted everyone to view me as Supermom. I wanted people to say of me, "I don't know how she does it."

One way I see this manifested in my own life (and in the lives of other moms) is that I don't accept the help of my husband. Sure, I might let him do some things, but I micromanage. I might leave the house and kids for a few hours but check in every thirty minutes. If he deviates from the plan, I might never trust him again. Surely our husbands can't know what's best for our kids, right? Moms are the caregivers. They just know.

Anne-Marie Slaughter says in her book *Unfinished Business* that our culture, for all of its progress on women in the workforce, actually fails to embrace equality in the home. We don't accept help from our husbands because we believe that women are largely more knowledgeable and more competent in the domestic sphere. Slaughter's husband was the primary parent in the home. As a result, her sons sometimes wanted their father more than they wanted her: "If I am honest with myself, the hardest emotion to work through when I heard our son call for Andy rather than for me was not guilt but envy. Even with all the rewards of my career, I would still like them to call for me first."[6]

I can relate. When our third son was born, my husband spent a lot of time with our twin boys while I recovered and took care of the baby. My husband has always been a very hands-on parent. But what I struggled with most in those early weeks was a mix of guilt and jealousy over the fact that they didn't cry for me nearly as much as they cried for him. I felt like I had let them down. I had nothing to live for if I wasn't the one they longed for. This type of thinking is dangerous and unhelpful for us in our work. We are important, yes. And depending on the age of our children, we are their very source of life. But a mother is not the only person they need. Acknowledging our limitations, taking intentional times of rest from our work, and even giving them breaks from their own contributions to the work teaches our children the value of Sabbath rest and points them to the Christ who is our true rest.

There is no question that men and women behave differently in the home. But that doesn't mean that both are not valuable contributors to at-home work. We have done a great disservice to families in the Christian community as we have elevated the Proverbs 31 woman to saint status. She is praised for her tireless work, yet we forget to mention that she had servants. She was no more a supermom than we are. Her place in Scripture is not to tell us how to be the mom of the century. Accepting help from our friends, our husbands, our parents, and anyone else who wants to lend a helping hand is not accepting defeat. It's God's gift of rest to you. Take it. Embrace it. And let the rest go.

Before I move on, let me say that I am terrible at this. I struggle with the supermom temptation as much as the next woman. But I know I can't keep up the pace of my own life. I can't take care of three kids under three while also taking care of my home perfectly. God never intended me to. He gave me a husband. He gave me friends and the body of Christ. In order to find rest in our work, we need to reorient our thinking about who should be doing the work of the home and then allow other people who love us and our children to do their part.

Idleness in Our Work

My mom often tells us how regularly she was asked, "Just what do you do all day?" Whenever we find ourselves in the trenches of the mommy wars, someone (either in jest or sincerity) brings up the stereotype that a stay-at-home mom watches soap operas and eats bon-bons while lounging on the couch all day.

I know a lot of stay-at-home moms, and I don't know any who fit that bill. But I'm going to risk entering dangerous territory here. While the caricature that stay-at-home moms don't do anything all day long is categorically untrue, we do face a unique temptation to fritter the hours away on meaningless things. Depending on our season of life, many things vie for our attention and few boundaries keep us from them.

I know that for all the moms who struggle with sitting down and resting from the work that consumes them, there are plenty who struggle with actually starting the work that needs to get done. As we saw in chapter 1, the work of the home has changed in its scope and expectation as our world has become more industrialized and efficient. A stay-at-home mom one hundred years ago had less downtime than a stay-at-home mom does today. I'm not saying downtime is bad. The advances we have seen in our society have made our work easier, and I'm thankful for that. No one is arguing that we go back to the days of churning our own butter, sewing our own clothes (out of necessity), and plucking the chickens for the evening meal. But modern advancements have given us time to spare (depending on our season). Not all moms have time to spare in the day. But some do, and the question we need to ask ourselves is, are we using that discretionary time for endless leisure or concentrated times of work and rest?

When you have no boss looking over your shoulder (unless you count your three-year-old demanding his third glass of milk), no scheduled hours to complete, and no projects on the horizon, it is easy to slip into seasons of idleness. While I struggle with making work an idol, I find myself falling into ruts of idleness too. This looks different for different people and at different seasons of life, but we must all be mindful of the reality that our current technologically connected culture makes slipping into idleness easy for us. Let's face it, a lot of days it seems far more inviting to put our comfy pants on and binge watch our favorite show on Netflix instead of making snacks for the upcoming youth group party. And sometimes we need that. But other times we need to do the hard thing in our work, even when our couch is calling our name.

A tension exists between making work an idol and being idle in our work. And every person's capacity and life is different, so it is not an easy line to distinguish. Ask a friend or your husband how you relate to work. Are you in danger of making it an idol? Or are you idle? Then ask God to give you the grace to balance the tasks of your life with your need for rest.

The Work Is Ever Before You

Another challenge to resting in our work is that there are no clear distinctions between work and home. When your home is your work, how do you rest? When your children don't operate on a nine-to-five schedule, is rest even possible?

Not only have we made home a function of our identity, but we have also made home a place of refuge, where we recharge after a hard day's work. Many of us who spent years working outside of the home used to view the evenings and weekends as times to recharge. But what happens when the dishes are piled in the sink from breakfast, the trash is overflowing, and the kids need to be shuttled to various practices? You can't retreat to your bedroom for a cup of tea and a good book. Work must be done often into the evening even after you've put in hours elsewhere (or even worked all day at home). A culture that values leisure makes seeing the home as a place of productivity and hard work difficult. How do you rest when you work where you live, when your job is your home?

I asked my friend Hannah how she incorporates rest into her life. She is a pastor's wife, mother, writer, and speaker, so rest is hard for her. But in spite of the many ways she is pulled to continue working from sunup to sundown, here is how she finds rest when the unfinished work is before her:

> You must intentionally step away from the work and leave it undone. For example, my mother-in-law never cooked on Sunday. My husband grew up with PB&J sandwiches or leftovers. We've adopted that in our family, and it's one of the best things ever. Knowing that I'm not responsible to cook meals on Sunday, as minor as it is, frees me to enter the day a little less stressed. As a pastor's family, we still have a lot happening on Sunday, but a big dinner is not one

of them. Dishes also don't get done until Sunday night. We stack them in the sink without guilt and head off to have a quiet Sunday afternoon. Later, when we're getting ready for bed, we'll set up the dishwasher to run overnight; but before then, we don't worry about them one bit.

Kevin DeYoung calls this "working hard at rest."[7] When we think about rest, we think of it as leisure and a chance to be free from the constraints of work. And while some of it is leisure, it still takes effort on our part. We live in a fallen world where work is never done, so in order to obey the command to rest, we are going to need to let go of the unfinished work, enjoy what has already been completed, and rest in the God who is holding all of our chaotic unfinished business together by his Word (Col. 1:17; Heb. 1:3).

Work Versus Play

Within this discussion of work being a fluid part of our life, with no real beginning and end, a question keeps coming up in my own mind, and maybe yours as well. What is the difference between rest and play? Is it resting to read a book to your child? Is it resting to eat dinner when you open your home for hospitality? It can be difficult to discern what is work and what is play when it all melds together. But if work is about people, our rest is as well. Just as we are tempted to view our work as done for our own glory, we are tempted to view our rest the very same way. I see this in my own life when I lament my lack of rest, when what I really mean is that I haven't had a break from my kids in a while. I can rest while watching a show with them. I can rest while playing soccer with them outside. I can rest while eating dinner with them. Sometimes rest is watching Netflix by myself, and sometimes rest is eating pizza in the living room with my kids.

Kevin DeYoung says that "effective love is rarely efficient. People take time. Relationships are messy."[8] Anyone who spends any amount of time investing in people knows this to be true. He's not saying we don't rest when our work involves people; he is simply saying that a people-oriented life might change the way our rest looks sometimes—or might make us even busier than we intended to be. He goes on to say, "Stewarding my time is not about selfishly pursuing only the things I like to do. It's about effectively serving others in the ways I'm best able to serve and in the ways I am most uniquely called to serve."[9] For so long I assumed that I can only rest when I am doing the things that I want to do, the things I find restful. But rest is sometimes about enjoying my kids, enjoying the fruit of my labors. We view rest and work as things that exist for us. But they don't.

Rest Is a Means of Loving My Neighbor

Marva Dawn, author of *Keeping the Sabbath Wholly*, says that this view of rest actually frees us to love people more, because we aren't seeing them as a means to an end. She writes, "When we are not under the compulsion to be productive, we are given the time to dwell with others, to *be* with them and thereby to discover who they are."[10] Rest is about people as much as work is. People are not efficient, and sometimes they can be draining, but they are part of our Sabbath rest.

She goes on to say that the community is our accountability in this Sabbath rest. We can serve our fellow believers in their quest for rest and ceasing from work in helping them with chores around their home, participating in a restful activity together, and even encouraging the weary to sleep.[11] This is another reminder that along with the work, the rest from the work is a community effort. Left to ourselves we would either be lazy or workaholics.

By embracing time in our Sabbath rest we are free to love others in our resting. We are not bound to productivity or a schedule, so people are not a hindrance to those things. Dawn says that if we are resting in God's grace, we can fold others into that freedom also.[12] Our children can interrupt us, but it doesn't derail our day. Our neighbor can need help moving a piece of furniture, and we can joyfully serve. In our resting we are not a slave to the clock. In Christ we are free to serve because he is the Lord of the Sabbath, not vice versa. Dawn goes on to say that this ceasing opens us up for inefficient things like "sitting quietly together and enjoying each other's company."[13] Without the demands of life and work, we aren't blinded to the people in front of us. Rest gives us the chance to value the people we labor for on a daily basis.

While we might cease from work in our rest, we do not cease from delight. Our resting makes way for feasting. Our ceasing makes way for embracing and loving others. This requires a shift in our thinking. Work and rest are about loving our neighbor. Work and rest are about worshiping God and enjoying the good things he has given us. Balance is needed, that is for sure. Personality types and seasons of life determine how much individual rest we need. But it's not all about our own personal gratification. Sometimes our rest includes others (like playing with our children) and sometimes it's just us. But it is always about God.

Finding Our True Rest

Do you ever look at your day and wonder how you will get everything done? Or maybe you are a planner like me, and you look at your month or year and break out in a sweat. So many obligations, so little time. Or maybe your challenges are a different animal entirely. You want to rest too much. You look at the tasks, and it seems hopeless to get them all done so you spend all afternoon on Pinterest or Facebook. The answer for every challenge we face to rest from our work is the same—Jesus is our rest.

The prevailing theme regarding rest in Scripture is that rest is a creation ordinance. Because God rested, so should we. But like I already said, God rested as a sign of completion. We don't get that luxury. We still are required to rest even when the work is not all done. This is where understanding the rest that Jesus provides us is so helpful. It carries life-giving hope for the parent who is prone to idleness in work and the one prone to idolatry. For the couch potato and the supermom.

This side of heaven we will always face the tension of incomplete work in the midst of rest. When we finally enter that eternal rest that our weary souls long for, there will be no more incomplete to-do lists because the greatest task that we have yet to accomplish will be complete. We will be with Jesus. We will have new eyes to see him as he is (1 John 3:2). We will be free of sin, idolatry, and idleness. And we will have rest.

Even as we struggle through the command to rest in our work that never ends, there is another challenge to our work that is just as vicious. Guilt. It is a problem that plagues us all, so that is where we are headed in the next chapter.

Getting Practical

Sometimes it's hard to rest when the work is ever before you. Emily, a homeschooling mom of three, is regularly reminded of the work she can't get done. Laundry overflows, but she has no time to fold it. Dirty dishes creep from the sink to the counter, leading her to feel overwhelmed and paralyzed, unable to begin the process of digging out from the mess. She doesn't like when her life gets too busy to keep up with the daily tasks, but for the last year her life has gotten chaotic. "Being a homemaker is a full-time job," she told me. "And because my kids are home all day long, keeping up with the work is a priority." But she can't always do that. Some weeks she must choose between watching a movie with her husband or finishing the dinner dishes, or between a playdate with a good friend or folding the laundry from yesterday. Most of the at-home work of her tiny house for five messy people falls on her, and it's overwhelming. She's often stuck between finding time to rest and finishing the task that is right in front of her.

Can you relate? Do you find yourself overwhelmed by the workload or longing for the rest that never comes? How can you intentionally rest even when the work is ever before you?

7

Am I Getting Fired?

I've been fired once. I didn't enjoy the job to begin with, but it was rather humiliating walking out of the building when everyone knew I should have been working my scheduled shift. To make matters worse, I was fired over a scheduling mishap. I said I couldn't work a certain shift, I was scheduled the shift, and I missed the shift. So there I was, walking the walk of shame out of the building and out into the cold parking lot—jobless and embarrassed.

Being fired carries with it a stigma of failure, of not measuring up, of laziness. No one wants to be fired from a job. In fact, we even have terminology for the various ways people can lose their jobs. *Fired. Laid off. Downsized. Reduction in force. Let go.* Sometimes people lose their jobs because of no fault of their own. And sometimes they don't meet the requirements of the job.

Do you ever wonder if you meet the requirements of your job? Do you wonder if you measure up to your ideal for your work?

Are you fearful of those same shameful feelings that I felt when I got fired? If I'm truly honest, even after a hard day's work, I feel similar embarrassment over what I did (or didn't) do on a given day. Was it enough? Did I do the right things?

After all of the talk so far about the purpose of our work, and even our need to rest from our work, there is a topic that gnaws at all of us on a daily basis—guilt. What I hope to do in this chapter is show how and why guilt in our work eats at us, and then I will present a practical and scriptural path away from guilt to freedom.

In an episode of *The Mindy Project*, which provided some good material to think through during its fourth season, the main characters, Mindy and Danny, finally come to a head on whether she will stay home with their son. Danny comes to the conclusion that Mindy is selfish for wanting to leave their son to go back to work. She tells him that any time they talk about their son and her work choices, it is always a commentary on her character, her identity. In his mind, any choice she makes is directly related to her being a mom to her son, and therefore the stakes are higher. Either way, the identity is rooted in what she does. She's a good mom if she stays home. She's a good doctor if she goes back to work. But in all of it, how she is viewed is tied to her work.[1]

We all struggle with finding our identity in our work, but it stings a bit more when it relates to the work of the home, doesn't it? Unfinished dishes are an attack on our ability to be a good housewife. A rebellious kid speaks to our parenting. Even a yard that is not mowed testifies to some degree of laziness we fear as we ponder what the neighbors might be thinking about our unkempt yard.

We are also at the mercy of an unrealistic ideal that has been set up for us for a long time. We are all on a quest to be the perfect homemaker, yet no one really knows who she is. And no one knows how to become her.

Who's the Boss?

One of the first challenges we face in our work, especially if we went from working in a setting where we had a clearly defined boss and authority structure, is that now we don't have a boss. For the most part the work is left up to us to divvy up (and often do ourselves). And like the loss of clear community and collaboration in our work, the loss of a clearly defined boss can be hard for some people.

In her book *Fit to Burst*, Rachel Jankovic says, "When you are a mother and a homemaker, you are your own boss. The days are what you make of them. The tasks that need to get done are put on a list at your discretion."[2]

So what happens when things don't get done? You have a long list at the start of your day that gets derailed by a fussy baby, a sick child home from school, or a friend who needs a cup of coffee and a listening ear. Or what if things get done at the expense of someone else? Your children, neighbor, or spouse need you, yet so do the dishes and the laundry and the baseboards. Maybe you are caring for a sick relative, and it feels like you have multiple bosses (the kids, the spouse, the physical work of the home, and the relative). There is never enough time, never enough energy, and never enough resources to get everything done. And because you are your own boss, you are your worst boss too. Depending on your personality, you can either turn that confusion over who your supervisor is into an overachieving response to guilt or you can resign yourself to defeat and wallow in self-pity. Either way, the guilt lingers. But not having a boss isn't the only thing that contributes to our guilty feelings.

A Limitless Job Description

Michael Horton says that "nowhere is the ordinary more important to culture, and yet less valuable in our society than in relation to motherhood."[3]

Because of this, and a whole host of other reasons, it's hard to pin down a job description for at-home work. No one gives you a manual when you bring the baby home from the hospital. No one, besides lifestyle magazines and cooking shows, tells you how to get things done around the house (and even then it's generic and not tailored to your home or experience). No one tells you how to care for a dying spouse or a sick parent. No one tells you how to organize the PTA fundraiser or plant grass or fix a faucet. But every one of these things typically falls under at-home work—among a myriad of other things.

I had a job once that had no job description. At first it was appealing. I could make the job what I wanted it to be. I could expand it based on my gifts and my interests. The sky was the limit. But what happened was that my sky eventually bumped up against my boss's sky, and my job became that of overpaid assistant rather than qualified colleague. I was no longer being used as a team member, there to help meet a common goal. I was bored, aimless, and often felt like I wasn't doing enough, because in reality I never knew what I was supposed to be doing in the first place.

This is how at-home work can be sometimes. Of course we know that the dishes need to be done and that the kids need to be fed. But we don't know what comes first sometimes. We don't know how to measure the importance of any given task, and therefore find ourselves ashamed when we don't get everything done. Because we have no real boss, who do we ask about the unfinished tasks of a given day? Who do we collaborate with on the seemingly limitless job description that is at-home work? It can be an isolating, lonely, and overwhelming experience sometimes. Add to that the fact that there are many days when we can't quantify what we actually did all day, and the guilt is only magnified.

Michael Horton goes on to say:

> Many of the things that mothers do in the home are not even measurable, much less stupendously satisfying on a daily basis. Much of it can be tedious, repetitive, and devoid of the intellectual stimulation found in adult company. In a myriad of ways, the daily calling of dying to self is felt more acutely by mothers. What they need is fewer guilt trips and expectations and more encouragement as they invest in ordinary tasks that yield long-term dividends. . . . Yet there is no promotion in motherhood. Successes are measured in years, not days or even months, and you can never be quite sure of all the things you did each day that made a difference. Mothers stand at the core of that gift exchange as it radiates into ever-wider concentric circles, from the home to the neighborhood and church, and to society at large. Precisely because they are gifts and not commodities, domestic labors sustain communities that cannot be measured or valued in the marketplace. That is their strength, not their weakness.[4]

This is where all we've seen comes to a head. We can't quantify the value of the work. We don't know how we are doing on any given day. Couple this with the disillusionment we've already talked about, and it makes us feel guilty and confused. The limitless job description that has no real beginning and end takes its toll on anyone whose primary work is in the home. And it's compounded by another ever-present foe in our fight against guilt.

Having It All

We are all familiar with the debate about whether women can have it all. We've been having it for a long time. Often the debate is limited to the working woman, the one who is trying to juggle work and family and wonders if it is possible to do it all well. The temptation for those who work in the home is to think that this debate doesn't pertain to them. You aren't trying to have it all. In fact, you gave up having it all in order to stay home. The very fact that you are a stay-at-home mom proves that you are not part of this debate.

But I beg to differ.

Sure, we may not be trying to have it all out in the market-place, but we most certainly are tempted to try to have it all in the home. Let me explain with a story.

When I was a new wife, I wrongly believed that to be a good wife I needed to do everything in the home. If my husband had to so much as fold his underwear, I was failing in my responsibilities to him. But I worked a full-time job. He was in seminary and working part time, so his time was as maxed out as mine was. In a lot of ways we were both just hanging on, leaving much of the work of the home (or apartment in our case) to the weekend and evenings. It was a joint effort, and I often felt like a failure when he did his share. Fast forward a few years to when I became a stay-at-home mom: my feelings of failure only intensified when I became a mom to not one, but two babies. Twins throw most couples for a loop, and we were no exception. I remember talking to an older twin mom once we had emerged from the newborn fog, and she said to me, "You have the benefit of having twins on the front end of having babies. It will make your husband more helpful because he had to help so much with the twins." I can attest to this. My husband is as much involved with the twins as he is with the housework. To make it even more difficult for my stereotype-loving self to accept, he actually likes the housework and time with our kids. It's a blessing, I know. But one woman's struggle is another woman's treasure, and I confess that I feel like a failure if I'm not superwoman. And I'm not.

In fact, for a long time I felt that if I wasn't doing everything, then I couldn't justify my existence at home. That's what a stay-at-home mom does, right? She can do everything. She can get the dishwasher loaded, the breakfast made (from scratch!), the laundry folded (and put away!), and keep the floors sparkling all while teaching her children the ABCs and a weekly Bible verse. She can also host her neighbors for dinner, plan a Bible study, and exercise regularly. Does that make you exhausted? It does me. Does that make you feel guilty? Me too. The myth of having it all is alive and well in the home today. We may not want to have it all in the marketplace, but we sure do want to say we can have it all within the walls of our homes.

Over time I have had to confess that I am not God. I'm not able to do all things well. I'm not going to be my family's savior. Only Jesus can be that. And my husband's willingness and ability to help is a gift to me, not a slight against my womanhood (more on that in a little bit). I am a limited, finite being made to realize that I cannot do everything I want to (or even need to) on a given day. I shouldn't feel guilt about that. It should actually lead me to depend more on the God who has it all and has given his gifts to me freely.

Even culture has picked up on these unrealistic at-home work expectations. In an episode of *The Mindy Project*, after Mindy tells her fiancé, Danny, that he doesn't understand what the work involves every day, he decides to take a stab at it—and is exhaustedly surprised at how even the smallest thing can derail the best laid plans for productivity on a given day. He recognizes that the endless quest to do it all is often met with surprising resistance from the smallest person in his home—his son.

In our Christian subculture we elevate the Proverbs 31 woman as the model for getting things done. Translate that into our isolated American context, and we are left trying to be superwoman, ignoring the fact that homemaker perfection is not the point of that passage. The point of the passage is to highlight the very things that Proverbs talks about throughout the book—wisdom. The wise woman manages her home well, but she doesn't do it perfectly. She can't do it alone. And she most certainly can't do it all. As I already said, let's not forget that she had servants.

The Comparison Trap

Contributing to our feelings of guilt is the temptation to compare ourselves to others. We compare ourselves to the mother who has more or fewer children than us. We compare ourselves to the family with the nicer house, the newer car, more disposable income, or more godly children. We compare ourselves to the crafty mom, the gourmet cook mom, the busy mom, the relaxed mom, the happy mom, the organized mom, and on and on and on. But these are just stereotypes. Our comparison leads to envy and discontentment. And guilt.

Author Emily Wierenga says this about our guilt:

> Competition keeps us feeling guilty. (The Playground is the playing field. Does she breastfeed? Does she clean every day? Does she ever take a break? Does she read to her kids? Play with her kids? Make her own baby food? Vaccinate? Mow the grass?) It's never enough.

We need a perfect home, perfect children, so we never stop working. We can't enjoy the home because we are always trying to live up to an ideal.[5]

Surely you have felt those same feelings before. I know I have.

So how do we fight this? It's easy to brush off our competitive spirit as just a mother's love (some of it might be), but it's more than that. And it's not unique to us. Peter faced the same temptation (John 21:20–22). When the Savior foretold Peter's story, Peter's heart immediately turned to comparison. *Lord, what about this man?* As swiftly as those words rolled off his tongue, Jesus responded to him with words for us to live by: *What is that to you? You follow me.*

Jesus knows our tendency toward comparison. He knows our bent toward envy and pride over what we are doing, and he says something simple yet profound. *Follow me. Never mind what he is doing, Peter. You follow me alone.* We will always encounter people who are better than us, smarter than us, craftier than us, and more patient than us. Such women will probably be better at keeping things organized than us and they may (on the outside) look like they have it all. That's not our business. And the only way we will avoid the comparison trap is to turn from it completely and follow the Savior who died to make our efforts an offering of praise to the Father, no matter how small they may be. We don't need to compare ourselves to the stay-at-home mom next door or in our Bible study. Her race is not our own. We have not been given her gifts or God's specific grace for her life; therefore we have no room to compare or boast in what we have that she doesn't or what we lack that she has. It's all of grace and all for our good. We are simply called to run the race God has placed before us with faithfulness and joy (Col. 3:23; Heb. 12:1).

Fighting comparison is one step on a path to ridding ourselves of the guilt that weighs us down in our work. Understanding that the people around us are not in competition with us, but actually assets to our work, is the key to fighting comparison. God has placed them in our lives for our good, not our destruction. I saw this play out clearly as I talked to Leanne about her work as a full-time house parent to kids from difficult backgrounds. I'll let her story of freedom from guilt and comparison speak:

> In the beginning I really battled being supermom, because in my mind, with being "paid" to be a mom, I felt like I needed to parent perfectly. I felt like eyes were always on my kids and me. It took going to counseling and lots of time on my knees for me to be released from these thoughts. With parenting at the ranch, there are a lot of people who have their hands in your parenting. Your boss, the social workers, the therapist, the childcare team . . . and the list goes on. I allowed that to cripple me and hinder me in having freedom in the way I felt led to parent. The Lord helped me shift my focus to allowing the circumstance to help me grow as a parent. I started seeing all these people as resources to my parenting instead of judges of the way I was parenting. I spoke candidly to them and asked for advice. Through the nature of the position, they were forced into my life as a mom—but it wasn't until I was intentional about opening up my life and heart to their advice that I saw it as a huge resource. Now that I am outside of the ranch and "professional parenting," I still want to surround myself with people who I can let into my life as a mom. I want to do this for accountability as well as encouragement. It is vital that we have people who not only encourage us, but also spur us on to be the best moms we can be because it is tempting

to cocoon ourselves and not grow in our role as mothers. It is important to process with other people because there are so many times we will not get it right and we need others to help us see those times.

This battle of comparison is an ongoing process. You may move beyond the guilt over not reading to your toddler as much as the next mom only to be met with feelings of failure for not joining the PTA or leading the high school bake sale. New seasons bring new opportunities to battle comparison and guilt.

Fighting Guilt

As we move from understanding why we feel guilty in our work to our hope for change, we need to first distinguish between true guilt and false guilt. Our strongest weapon in fighting guilt is to understand what our guilt is telling us in the first place. Second Corinthians 7:5–13 looks at the difference between "godly grief" and "wordly grief." We could call this grief *guilt*. We all struggle with guilt to some degree; the challenge is discerning where that guilt is coming from and what that guilt is saying about us. Paul would say that godly guilt has one clear purpose: repentance. The end result of our guilt should be repentance (v. 10), which means that true, godly guilt is a direct result of sin in our life. Godly grief (guilt) produces a host of fruit in our life; it produces a desire for change that leads to growth in godliness; and it produces a zeal for holiness (v. 11). Another purpose for godly guilt is that others may witness such a profound transformation (vv. 9, 13). And there is a clear direction for godly grief and guilt—heavenward. It moves us away from ourselves and to the God who is true, right, and good.

John Piper says this about what he calls misplaced and well-placed shame:

Misplaced shame (the kind we ought *not* to have) is the shame you feel when there is no good reason to feel it. Biblically that means that the thing you feel ashamed of is not dishonoring to God; or that it *is* dishonoring to God, but you didn't have a hand in it. In other words, misplaced shame is shame for something that's good—something that doesn't dishonor God. . . .

Well-placed shame (the kind we *ought* to have) is the shame we feel when there is good reason to feel it. Biblically that means we feel ashamed of something because our involvement in it was dishonoring to God. We ought to feel shame when we have a hand in bringing dishonor upon God by our attitudes and actions.

Much of what makes us feel shame is not that we have brought dishonor to God by our actions, but that we have failed to give the appearance that other people admire. Much of our shame is not God-centered but self-centered.[6]

Have you ever stopped to think that much of the guilt you feel in your work at home is actually a result of judging your work on the merits of something other than God and his Word? There is no freedom from guilt that comes from anywhere other than a place of repentance over sin. Where there is no sin, there should be no guilt. But so often we feel shame and guilt-ridden over a myriad of things that are not directly related to God's glory.

What does this look like when we are weighed down with guilt in our work? *Guilt over not doing enough. Guilt over not being superwoman. Guilt over not being able to have it all. Guilt over your sinful comparison to someone else. Guilt over not measuring up to an unrealistic job description. Guilt over what others may think of how you do your work. Guilt over being too clean and organized. Guilt for being too messy. Guilt for being scheduled. Guilt for being flexible.*

The list could go on and on. And we all need a path of escape from it all.

First, discern if the guilt is from true sin or if it is from something else (like cultural pressure, unrealistic expectations, or too much introspection). If it is not true sin, then it's not godly guilt and needs no repentance from you. You are free to live as you are without fear over whether your work is enough. It is. If it is owing to true sin, there is so much hope for you in Jesus. Confess your sin; he will be faithful to forgive it, cleanse you from unrighteousness, and provide you with the grace to do better the next time.

Now that we've talked about how to identify where the guilt is coming from, we can move forward with practical steps in not letting guilt rule over us in our work.

Let the Men Help

As I talked about in chapters 4 and 5, the home is for everyone. It's for everyone, and it's a community effort. If it matters that the kids are helping, then it matters that our husbands help too. For a long time the work of the home has been brushed aside as "women's work." As one who sees my home as my primary responsibility, I see how this happens. But the biblical commands pertaining to child-rearing and hospitality are for both genders. Fathers are specifically commanded not to exasperate their children, which shows they are involved with their children (Eph. 6:4). Elders are specifically commanded to be hospitable (1 Tim. 3:2; Titus 1:8). Cleaning and caring for children is not for women only. I may be the lead parent in the home, my primary work may be my home, and my responsibility may make me the one who bears the majority weight of it all, but that does not mean that I'm the *sole* worker in the home. When the work of the home is for everyone, then our identity isn't destroyed when our husband helps around the house. We are able to understand and embrace that he is a contributor too.

A friend shared how she feels when her husband does anything around the house. Because the home is "her job," she feels like she alone must do it all:

> I often feel like my husband shouldn't have to do any of the domestic tasks because he has been working all day—and I haven't, or at least not as much or as hard (so I think). So I feel guilty when he does the dishes or sweeps the floor or takes out the trash. But the fact is, not every responsibility in the home is my responsibility, and a lot of times my husband is just trying to be kind and serve me. This should cause me to feel loved, not guilty.

As I talked about in the previous chapter, one of the ways we fight our sinfulness in our work is to let others help us. So how can husbands help?

It's not a "mom fail" if my husband watches the kids for a few hours while I go write, have coffee with a friend, or grocery shop alone. I won't get more jewels in my crown in heaven if I do it all by myself. In fact, my husband is just as responsible for the outcome of my kids' faith as I am. He is just as responsible for how our neighbors are loved by us as I am. He is just as responsible for bringing order out of chaos in the mundane and ordinary tasks of our home as I am. He may not do it as much as I do, but that doesn't change the fact that it takes a whole family to make a home.

The "who is doing it" debates have only increased these feelings of identity loss. We have made the home so much about our personal fulfillment and identity that when we let someone else do the work of the home, we feel as if our very self is being replaced or overshadowed.

Anne-Marie Slaughter says that "being needed *is* a universal desire and the traditional coin in which mothers have been compensated. . . . It is one thing to let go of the housekeeping. Quite another to relinquish being the center of your children's universe."[7]

Isn't that what we feel like we are losing when we let anything go? Slaughter goes on to say that this idea that mothers do everything is actually a newer phenomenon, one that came into existence only in the last one hundred years. Fathers traditionally have been as involved in the caregiving as mothers, just in different ways. In societies where farming is the key industry, everyone learns some aspect of the work of the home from both mother and father.[8] It is only when fathers left for work and mothers stayed home to raise the children that this sharp divide about who is doing the work emerged.

So let your husband help. Maybe he won't do certain tasks the way you would do them. (Who ever does things the same as another person, anyway?) But the home is his too. The kids are his too. You all are part of the collective unit called the home.

Be Faithful

At the end of the day, we will not be judged on how well we cleaned our floors, how many flowers we planted in our yard, how many activities our kids were involved in, or how many times we played trains on the floor with our three-year-old. Those things are good and beneficial, but they won't save us. What will mark us is faithfulness. Did we do our work "as for the Lord" (Col. 3:23–24) rather than for the praise of the mom or dad next door? Did we recognize true sin in our work, and did we repent of it? Did we acknowledge our finiteness and limitations and respond with humility to them? Being supermom isn't the fast track to heaven or the "good parent list." But faithfulness in the ordinary, even when it is hard, is true greatness. This faithfulness points to something we can't always see with our limited vision. It's part of something much grander than we often understand, which is the basis for our final chapter.

Getting Practical

Having four young children doesn't leave much time to decide who is doing the dishes or who is doing the baths. Both mom and dad are needed to get the house cleaned up and the kids to bed. When Miriam's husband, Perry, comes home from work and starts cleaning up or doing the dishes at the end of the night, guilt washes over her. Of course, she appreciates his help. There are a lot of little people in their house, and the work is more than she can handle sometimes. But it's hard for her not to feel like a "mom fail" when she sees him doing work that she sees as *her* work, not his. "If I see Perry doing laundry or dishes, my first thought is that he must think I'm not doing enough, and he probably thinks if he doesn't do it, it won't get done. I should be thankful that he gladly helps, but usually I just think I'm failing because I can't get everything done." If everyone is a contributor to the work of the home, then it's not an attack on your identity or your ability to do your job when your husband helps. He's simply playing his part in contributing to the work of the home.

How are you tempted to see help from others as an attack on your identity? What are some ways you can let go of the guilt you feel over not being able to do it all?

8

Our Work Is Taking
Us Somewhere

I've always wanted my life to count for something. Never one to be bored, I dreamed big and let my imagination run wild as a kid. This desire for importance continued into adulthood and parenthood. It's the proverbial question that often lingers in my mind (maybe yours too): *Does my work count for something? Am I making a difference in the world?*

I hope by now you are convinced that it does. In these final pages, though, I want to move us to an even broader understanding of how our work has value and counts for something bigger than ourselves. It's not just about the life we live right now, but the life that is to come.

After all of our talk about the need for others in our work, loving our neighbors in our work, what to do with the guilt we face in our work and the rest we need from our work, we end by considering God's great global purpose in our work—spreading his glory throughout the world. One of the ways he does that is through his body, the church (Matt. 28:18–20). We know that he spreads his glory through the local churches we all find ourselves in, but the local church also consists of individual members who have lives that they live day in day out. We carry that mission with us when we go into our respective fields of work—including the home. God's purposes are accomplished not just on Sunday morning, but also Monday through Saturday as we labor in our work. Throughout this book, I've continued to come back to the fact that our work is a means of loving God by loving our neighbor.

As we tie together everything we've learned from the previous chapters, I want to show the redemptive nature of the work by focusing on two key themes: it's for the world (loving God by loving neighbor), and it's also for eternity (future-oriented). The hope in our work as Christians is that we get to worship God through our work now, but we also are working in preparation for the better, glorified work to come in the new heavens and the new earth where we will worship him perfectly. I want us to look at where our work is taking us, both in the immediate, daily parts of our lives and in the future home we are awaiting. Our work is for the good of the world both now and in the world to come.

The Widow at Zarephath

It's easy to miss the tangible ways God is using our work to bless the world sometimes. It seems so mundane, so ordinary. Cooking a meal for a sick friend is so routine. Pulling weeds in the garden feels monotonous, but is the world a better place for it? Making our home a welcome place for guests is what we do, but are we really doing God's work in it? How is God working through our work to bless the world?

In 1 Kings 17 Elijah runs out of food. Elijah had prophesied that a drought would come to the land, and now he has no food or water. So God tells him to visit a widow whom he has commanded to feed him. Like everyone else in the land, this widow has very little, and even as Elijah journeys to her, she is preparing herself and her son to die (v. 12). Yet God does something miraculous in this moment. He feeds them and provides for them in greater abundance than they had before (v. 16). But do you want to know what is remarkable in this moment?

God provides for Elijah and her *by her work*.

God had a greater purpose in that moment than just meeting her physical needs. He was showing himself faithful to the widow and to Elijah. God was strengthening Elijah for the task at hand and caring for a poor widow and her son. God was revealing himself to a pagan woman as the one true God. It was through her ordinary work of baking a cake that the prophet was fed, her household gained food to last through the drought, and God was shown to be faithful. It was in her ordinary work that she, a Gentile, was given a category for God that prepared her for the loss she would experience just a few verses later when her son dies (1 Kings 17:17–24). While it seemed so ordinary— baking a cake when all hope for survival seemed lost—God was doing his work in the world.

The work of the home is not always in the spectacular, like God working a miracle through baking a cake. But it is always for the world. If work is a means of loving God by loving your neighbor, then every act of faithful work that you do is accomplishing just that. You are loving God and the world by caring for the people in your home.

Shaping a Culture

People sometimes say "the hand that rocks the cradle rules the world" to affirm the work that they do at home. It is true that the baby we rock will one day grow into an adult who will influence society. At the time of this writing, I have a five-month-old baby, and as I nurse him and rock him to sleep, I wonder, *Is my work preparing him to be a contributor to society? Who will he become?*

If we take the view that all work matters to its logical conclusion, then the work we do in shaping future workers, future contributors to society, is immensely important. Anne-Marie Slaughter, who has written extensively on caregiving and how it impacts society, divides how our culture views work into two spheres: competition and care. She says, "Competition produces money. But care produces people."[1] And it is caregiving that makes up the bulk of at-home work. The food is for people to eat. The sheets are for the beds that those people sleep in. The clean clothes are for them to wear. Care takes care of people, but care also shapes people.

But what about the Christian mother? How is a Christian mother able to take this work even a step further?

Sarah Edwards, wife of Jonathan Edwards, was a mother to eleven children, all of whom lived beyond childhood (rare in those days). Their children and descendants produced authors, college presidents, professors, doctors, politicians, pastors, missionaries, and many others that contributed to society. It all started with Sarah Edwards and her daily work in her home with her children, and from that work a nation has been shaped.[2] It is hard to quantify the lasting impact a Christian mother has on the culture, but Sarah Edwards gives us a glimpse. Her work was for the world.

Know Your Work

We don't all need to be doing the same thing, at the same capacity. That mind-set breeds false guilt (see chap. 7) or makes us all cookie-cutter versions of each other (which diminishes the creativity of God). The point of knowing how your work serves the world is driven home by knowing the work you are called to and knowing how your work matters in the grand scheme of things. Everyone has different gifts, capacities, and seasons, so there is no point in trying to fit at-home work into any one box.

Rachel Jankovic says this about finding the work that serves the world:

> We don't all need to be making biscuits, but we should all be doing something. We should be getting our hands into stuff to give. We should be blessing others, thinking of others, giving to others. And we should be doing it so freely that we don't remember it, because we are willing to wait to see what is done with it. We are willing to see, years down the road, what kind of interest accrued on those biscuits.[3]

Finding simple, tangible ways that your home can be used for the common good and doing that work faithfully is our aim. Even the most ordinary work, like cleaning the toilets, taking Christmas cookies to your neighbor, homeschooling your kids, inviting a weary friend over for lunch, walking your neighbor's dog, visiting an elderly relative in the nursing home, raking leaves, serving on the PTA, managing the estate of an aging parent, listening to your teenager after a hard day at school, or any other seemingly mundane things you do on a given day is serving the world through your home. Michael Horton says that when we begin seeing these ordinary actions as the "site of [God's] faithfulness, we will begin to appreciate our own calling to love and serve others in his name in everyday ways that make a real difference in people's lives."[4] Your work, whatever it is, is the site of God's faithfulness. It makes a difference in people's lives, even if it seems small.

In many ways, our goal is not to find a new purpose for our work, but to recognize that the work we are already called to, the work that is right in front of us, is God's good means of spreading his glory throughout the world. You are his image bearer, tasked with loving his fellow image bearers through the ordinary, faithful work that greets you every morning. This is for the good of the world.

When you feed your husband and children, you tangibly remind them that we have a God who meets all of our physical needs (Matt. 6:26). When you open your home to others, those you know and those you don't, you show your guests that God is a God who welcomes people into his home (John 14:2–3). When you take out the trash, you declare with your actions that the curse may rise up all around you, but it will one day be defeated once and for all (1 Cor. 15:57). These things may feel routine, and they are at times, but they are important; they allow others to see that God is involved in even the routine details of the world that he has made.

Leanne (whom you met in the last chapter) describes a tangible way her seemingly ordinary work is an act of loving God by loving her neighbor. I asked her how she sees her work as serving this greater purpose of being for the good of the world:

> I think my answer would've been different last week, but I had a pretty cool experience this past Sunday. We returned to our home church after living in another state for the last six years. The first evening we were back, a lady ran up to me and gave me a huge hug and told me her family had re-

ally missed me. She walked away, and my husband asked who she was. I had no idea. I later figured out that she was someone who was new to our Sunday school class seven years ago. I told my husband, "I took a meal to her once and spent about an hour or so getting to know her." I never realized how much a few servings of food and a short conversation would mean to someone (seven years later).

Many days I feel exhausted caring for my kids and all the upkeep of the house. I feel like I cannot provide for one more person, and then an experience like this reminds me that the Lord uses that service in mighty ways. The fact that I am home and can come up with creative ways to serve others while serving my family is a gift. Just recently my kids and I were coming up with ideas of ways we could serve others. We decided we could tack on a trip to a local widow each Tuesday when we go to the library, or double up on our meal servings to freeze a meal for someone in need. I think my favorite word right now is "intentional." We have to be intentional about everything we do—and when we are, the Lord is there working through our service.

Instead of trying to fit a particular mold, Leanne has asked God for eyes to see how her work is (and can be) for others right now. She is ordering her life with intentionality, so her kids and others will see God in her and so lives can be transformed by the love of Christ.

For the Good of the Future World

But this world is fleeting and fading. All of us want to know that what we are doing now has lasting impact on eternity, right? We get that our work is impacting souls who will never die (John 11:26). We get that loving our neighbor is a means of worshiping

God (Mark 12:30–31). But what does our work have to do with our future home, the new heavens and the new earth?

God created us to work. It was not an afterthought to him (Gen. 2:15). Work is not a result of the curse. It's woven into our personhood. The fact that we were created to work is a direct reflection of God, the one whose image we bear. God works, so we work, and because of this, work will not cease when we all get to heaven. It will simply be better, perfect, and unstained by sin.

I used to be rather terrified of heaven. I don't like being bored or having nothing to do, and in my faulty understanding, heaven was one big worship service where all people did was sing and play music while floating on clouds. I love to sing, but I thought it would get old after a while. I looked at the world around me, the work I enjoyed, the food I liked to eat, the people I loved talking with and being around, and I couldn't see how (even though I would be without sin and with Jesus) heaven was better than what was right in front me. I think a lot of people feel that way. We need a robust understanding of the new heavens and the new earth. Yes, we will be free from sin (hallelujah!), but we will also be part of a new *earth*. Think about the garden of Eden for a moment. What was included in it? Food, people, animals, beauty, work, and leisure. The things we love most in this world, the good gifts that God has given us, like our work, are only foretastes of the greater glory that awaits us when this old, cursed world passes away and a new one is born (Rev. 21:1). The mundane things of our day will be seen with glorified eyes to understand how they are fulfilling God's purposes in his creation. The thorns and thistles of our work (the never-ending laundry, the filthy kitchen, the rebellious children, the outrageous grocery prices) will be gone, and we will get all of the joy and none of the pain. The point of all of our work is to reflect the God who created us, to display his glory to a watching world, and to draw others to see it, too. In the new heavens and the new earth, we will be with God, so we will see and experience the purpose of our work in new and perfect ways because we will have bodies free from sin and we will be with the Redeemer (Isa. 65:17–25).

So how does our work now have any bearing on eternity, besides the impact on souls?

Pastor and author Tom Nelson has helped me to understand how my work now impacts my work later. He uses the parable of the talents (Matt. 25:14–30):

> In the parable of the talents, Jesus paints for us an enticing and hopeful picture of a future that brings with it great reward for diligence and faithfulness. Our future reward involves a joyful intimacy with God. We will "enter into the joy of our Master," but we will also be given greater work to do in the future. In many ways we are training now for reigning later with Jesus. The work you do now matters more than you often realize.[5]

He goes on to say that if the new heavens and the new earth that Peter talks about in 2 Peter 3 really is a purified earth (and not burned up or destroyed), then our work has eternal value. God works through us, his image bearers, to restore his creation to its rightful state. We are all working toward that final day when God redeems all that has been lost, resurrects us from the dead, and restores the earth to sin-free perfection (Rom. 8:19–22; Rev. 21:1–5). Our work is preparing us to rule and reign with Christ in a new earth, where the curse is gone, and we will work for God's glory, always.

In the garden God gave Adam and Eve work to do. It was good work. They were to cultivate the ground, rule over the animals, and enjoy the beautiful world that God made. I imagine they also had the ability to understand how every part of their work pointed them back to the God who made them. There was no mundane task because they could see the purpose in the things we find ordinary. There was no conflict in their soul about serving one another because they knew who was their neighbor and gladly worked for the good of the other. We don't live in that world any longer. But we will one day. While we may be clouded by our own sin and the overarching curse of life in a fallen world, our work hasn't changed. It still serves the same purpose—worship of God, pointing back to God, and pointing us forward to the life that is coming.

A Shot at Redemption

In any work, we fall prey to forgetfulness. When I was a waitress in college, we had a term for someone who was overwhelmed on a busy night. She was "in the weeds." Weeds can sometimes grow so thick around us that we can't see anything else. But on our most coherent days, we all want to know that what we are doing matters now and in eternity.

Journalist Jennifer Senior sees this in parents all the time. People's lives suddenly become focused and intentional when they have children. They see life as moving them toward something when their children enter the world. They have hope. They have a shot at redemption, she says.[6] What seemed so meaningless before now doesn't seem that way anymore.

Christians know something on an even larger scale. We know that we aren't the ones redeeming the culture through our work. Only God can do that. But we are given the privilege to work alongside of him. We are part of his cosmic plan to save a people for himself and make all things new. Our mundane, self-sacrificing work is part of that effort. It's about people. It's about seeing beyond the walls of our homes and seeing how what we do on any given day is not just blessing the people in the home, but also blessing the world that he has made. And it's all bringing him glory. Our work isn't giving us any points with God, but it is telling the world about the God we worship. It's telling what we value most. It's telling what we hope in even when it is hard. Christians work differently, in every kind of work, because we work for the Lord (not others) and we work hopefully (for the future).

Your work might be ordinary, but it's filled with glory. Your work might be mundane, but it's taking you somewhere. Your work might be born out of blood, sweat, and tears (literally), but it's producing life in others for people who have eternity in front of them. It's good work. It's meaningful work. And it matters to God.

Getting Practical

Deb is an empty-nest mom. Her kids are all grown, married, and have children of their own. Her days look different now than they did with four children sitting around her table or raiding her refrigerator. Her parents are now gone, but she remembers their final days so clearly. She was their caregiver. Deb's life has been marked by this work, sacrificing for the good of others. She is wife to her husband, church member to her friends at church, and mom to me.

While there may have been days when it felt like her work was pointless, Deb's work is bearing fruit now in the lives of her children. Her children love her, appreciate the sacrifices she made, and remember how she made our home a home. The caregiving work she provided to her parents at the end of their lives made them feel loved, and it modeled Christlike service, even when they didn't always appreciate it. It bore fruit in the lives of her dying parents. This work, though mundane, is good work. It is preparing her for eternity. Her work may have been ordinary, but it has always been glorious. And it left a mark on me.

The cycle of care you provide to others will come full circle, propelling you forward to a brighter hope in Christ. How can you see your work right now as having an impact on eternity? How is work preparing you to rule and reign with Christ in the new earth?

Notes

Chapter 1: The Changing Nature of At-Home Work

1. Louise Story, "Background: Reporting on the Aspirations of Young Women," *The New York Times*, September 23, 2005, http://www.nytimes.com/2005/09/23/national/23women-sidebar.html.

2. Louise Story, "Many Women at Elite Colleges Set Career Path to Motherhood," *The New York Times*, September 20, 2005, http://www.nytimes.com/2005/09/20/us/many-women-at-elite-colleges-set-career-path-to-motherhood.html?_r=0/.

3. See, for example, Deborah A. Kahn, *The Huffington Post*, May 19, 2014, http://www.huffingtonpost.com/deborah-a-kahn/what-research-shows-about_b_5352149.html.

4. Paulette Light, "Why 43% of Women With Children Leave Their Jobs, and How to Get Them Back," *The Atlantic*, April 19, 2013, https://www.theatlantic.com/sexes/archive/2013/04/why-43-of-women-with-children-leave-their-jobs-and-how-to-get-them-back/275134/.

5. Carolyn McCulley and Nora Shank, *The Measure of Success: Uncovering the Biblical Perspective on Women, Work, and the Home* (Nashville: B&H, 2014), 36.

6. Ibid., 44.

7. Betty Friedan, *The Feminine Mystique* (New York: W. W. Norton, 1963), 91.

8. Ibid., 28.

9. Even with the busy lives that pull them between work and home, parents today spend more time with their kids than previous generations. Some studies show dads tripling the amount of time spent with their kids in comparison to their parents.

10. Helaine Olen, "A Truce in the 'Mommy Wars,'" *Salon*, March 15, 2006, http://www.salon.com/2006/03/15/mommy_wars/.

11. Newsweek Staff, "Mommy vs. Mommy," *Newsweek*, June 3, 1990, http://www.newsweek.com/mommy-vs-mommy-206132.

12. D'Vera Cohn and Andrea Caumont, "7 Key Findings about Stay-at-Home Moms," April 8, 2014, http://www.pewresearch.org/fact-tank /2014/04/08/7-key-findings-about-stay-at-home-moms/.

13. D'Vera Cohn, Gretchen Livingston, and Wendy Wang, "After Decades of Decline, a Rise in Stay-at-Home Mothers," *Pew Research*, April 8, 2014, http://www.pewsocialtrends.org/2014/04/08/after-decades-of -decline-a-rise-in-stay-at-home-mothers/.

14. Sue Shellenbarger, "At-Home Dads Make Parenting More of a 'Guy' Thing," *The Wall Street Journal*, January 22, 2013, http://www.wsj .com/articles/SB10001424127887324624404578255792399791294.

15. Liz Pardue-Schultz, "Unpopular Opinion: Being a Stay-at-Home Mother Is Not a Job," *XO Jane*, March 6, 2015, http://www.xojane .com/issues/being-a-stay-at-home-mom-is-not-a-job/.

16. Paul David Tripp, "Trading One Dramatic Resolution for 10,000 Little Ones," Desiring God website, December 29, 2013, http://www.desiring god.org/blog/posts/trading-one-dramatic-resolution-for-10-000-little -ones/.

17. Eugene Peterson, *A Long Obedience in the Same Direction: Discipleship in an Instant Society* (Downers Grove, IL: InterVarsity Press, 2000), 44.

Chapter 2: Is There Life out There?

1. Tim Keller with Katherine Leary Alsdorf, *Every Good Endeavor: Connecting Your Work to God's Work* (New York: Dutton, 2012), 48–49.

2. I get this idea from Martin Luther: "In his vocation one is not reaching up to God, but rather bends oneself down toward the world. When one does that, God's creative work is carried on. God's work of love takes form on earth, and that which is external witnesses to God's love." Quoted in Gustaf Wingren, *Luther on Vocation* (Eugene, OR: Wipf & Stock, 1957), 10.

3. Nate Green, "How to Get a Cheap Private Chef," http://www.thenate greenexperience.com/how-to-get-a-cheap-private-chef/, accessed April 7, 2016.

4. Anne Kadet, "New York City's Grocery Delivery Wars: Who's the Winner?," *The Wall Street Journal*, February 6, 2015, http://www.wsj .com/articles/new-york-citys-grocery-delivery-wars-whos-the-winner -1423250707.

5. Wednesday Martin, "The Captivity of Motherhood," *The Atlantic*, July 15, 2015, http://www.theatlantic.com/entertainment/archive/2015 /07/the-captivity-of-motherhood/398525/.

6. Keller, *Every Good Endeavor*, 49.

7. Ibid., 46.

8. Jenna Goudreau, "Why Stay-at-Home Moms Should Earn a $115,000 Salary," *Forbes*, May 2, 2011, http://www.forbes.com/sites/jenna goudreau/2011/05/02/why-stay-at-home-moms-should-earn-a-1150 00-salary/.

9. Jen Wilkin, "FAQ: Should I Pay an Allowance for Chores?," *The Beginning of Wisdom* (blog), April 16, 2015, http://jenwilkin.blogspot .com/2015/04/faq-should-i-pay-allowance-for-chores.html/.

10. Gene Edward Veith develops this theme in his book *God at Work: Your Christian Vocation in All of Life* (Wheaton, IL: Crossway, 2002).

11. Michael Horton, *Ordinary: Sustainable Faith in a Radical, Restless World* (Grand Rapids, MI: Zondervan, 2014), 14.

Chapter 3: What about the Chores?

1. This quote is often attributed to Shane Claiborne, but it actually was posted on a sign in a New Monastic community. Tish Harrison Warren quotes it in her blog post, "Courage in the Ordinary," *The Well Blog*, April 3, 2013, http://thewell.intervarsity.org/blog/courage -ordinary/.

2. Kim Bhasin and Patricia Laya, "26 Shockingly Offensive Vintage Ads," *Business Insider* website, June 14, 2011, http://www.businessinsider .com/vintage-sexist-and-racist-ads-2011-6?op=1/.

3. Elizabeth Broadbent, "What Normal Looks Like," *Scary Mommy* (blog), accessed April 7, 2016, https://www.scarymommy.com/what -normal-looks-like/.

4. Tim Keller with Katherine Leary Alsdorf, *Every Good Endeavor: Connecting Your Work to God's Work* (New York: Dutton, 2012), 49.

5. Kathleen Norris, *The Quotidian Mysteries: Laundry, Liturgy, and "Women's Work"* (Mahwah, NJ: Paulist Press, 1998), 21–22.

6. Keller, *Every Good Endeavor*, 59.

7. I am greatly indebted to Rachel Marie Stone's book, *Eat with Joy: Redeeming God's Gift of Food* (Downers Grove, IL: InterVarsity Press, 2013), for giving me clarity in this section. She explores the purpose of food, the problems we have with food, and the ways we can find joy in eating our food in much greater detail. If you want to study this topic further, I recommend her book.

8. Rachel Jankovic, *Fit to Burst: Abundance, Mayhem, and the Joys of Motherhood* (Moscow, ID: Canon Press, 2013), 63.

9. Edith Schaeffer, *The Hidden Art of Homemaking: Creative Ideas for Enriching Everyday Life* (London: Tyndale, 1971), 81.

10. Ibid., 88.

Chapter 4: My Home, My People

1. Jennifer Senior, *All Joy and No Fun: The Paradox of Modern Parenting* (New York: Ecco, 2014), 10.
2. Ibid., 154.
3. Ibid.
4. Gustaf Wingren, *Luther on Vocation* (Eugene, OR: Wipf & Stock, 1957). This whole idea of loving your neighbor through work is taken from Wingren's book on Luther. It was the key idea that shaped Luther's understanding of vocation.
5. Martin Luther quoted in Wingren, *Luther on Vocation*, 120.
6. Ibid., 5.
7. Martin Luther, "The Estate of Marriage," sermon, https://www.1215.org/lawnotes/misc/marriage/martin-luther-estate-of-marriage.pdf, accessed April 27, 2016.
8. Jen Wilkin expands on this in "FAQ: Should I Pay an Allowance for Chores?," *The Beginning of Wisdom* (blog), April 16, 2015, http://jenwilkin.blogspot.com/2015/04/faq-should-i-pay-allowance-for-chores.html.
9. Michael Horton, *Ordinary: Sustainable Faith in a Radical, Restless World* (Grand Rapids, MI: Zondervan, 2014), 149.
10. Kathleen Norris, *The Quotidian Mysteries: Laundry, Liturgy, and "Women's Work"* (Mahwah, NJ: Paulist Press, 1998), 67.
11. Wingren, *Luther on Vocation*, 33.

Chapter 5: It Takes a Village

1. "For a Year, Shonda Rimes said 'Yes' to All Things That Scared Her," *All Things Considered*, November 9, 2015, http://www.npr.org/2015/11/09/455340952/for-one-year-shonda-rhimes-said-yes-to-all-the-things-that-scared-her/.
2. Jennifer Miller, "Growing Families That Stay Put," *The New York Times* website, October 25, 2015, http://www.nytimes.com/2015/10/25/realestate/large-families-in-tiny-apartments-for-the-sake-of-the-kids-friendships.html?_r=0/.
3. Sam Laird, "The Rise of the Mommy Blogger (info graphic)," *Mashable*, accessed April 7, 2016, http://mashable.com/2012/05/08/mommy-blogger-infographic/#LjZVa.5L5kq1.
4. Gene Edward Veith, *God at Work: Your Christian Vocation in All of Life* (Wheaton, IL: Crossway, 2002), 41.
5. Heather Davis Nelson, "Day 4: It Takes a Village (to Raise Twins)," *Hidden Glory* (blog), October 5, 2015, http://heatherdavisnelson.com/2015/10/05/day-4-it-takes-a-village-to-raise-twins/.
6. Hannah Anderson, email message to author, November 4, 2015.

Chapter 6: Miles to Go before I Sleep

1. See Robert Frost, "Stopping by Woods on a Snowy Evening," 1923, http://www.poetryfoundation.org/poem/171621.
2. J. I. Packer, *Weakness Is the Way: Life with Christ Our Strength* (Wheaton, IL: Crossway, 2013), 15–16.
3. Greg Gilbert and Sebastian Traeger, *The Gospel at Work: How Working for King Jesus Gives Purpose and Meaning to Our Jobs* (Grand Rapids, MI: Zondervan, 2013), 16.
4. Tim Keller with Katherine Leary Alsdorf, *Every Good Endeavor: Connecting Your Work to God's Work* (New York: Dutton, 2012), 40.
5. D. A. Carson, "Leaning Forward in the Dark: A Failed Reformation," sermon, June 30, 2014, http://resources.thegospelcoalition.org/library/leaning-forward-in-the-dark/.
6. Anne-Marie Slaughter, *Unfinished Business: Women, Men, Work, Family* (New York: Random House, 2015), 156.
7. Kevin DeYoung, *Crazy Busy: A (Mercifully) Short Book about a (Really) Big Problem* (Wheaton, IL: Crossway, 2013), 98.
8. Ibid., 105.
9. Ibid., 61.
10. Marva Dawn, *Keeping the Sabbath Wholly: Ceasing, Resting, Embracing, Feasting* (Grand Rapids, MI: Eerdmans, 1989), 20.
11. Ibid., 71.
12. Ibid., 122.
13. Ibid., 19.

Chapter 7: Am I Getting Fired?

1. *The Mindy Project*, "The Parent Trap," season 4, episode 12, aired December 1, 2015.
2. Rachel Jankovic, *Fit to Burst: Abundance, Mayhem, and the Joys of Motherhood* (Moscow, ID: Canon Press, 2013), 29.
3. Michael Horton, *Ordinary: Sustainable Faith in a Radical, Restless World* (Grand Rapids, MI: Zondervan, 2014), 192.
4. Ibid., 193.
5. Emily Wierenga, *Making It Home: Finding My Way to Peace, Identity, and Purpose* (Grand Rapids, MI: Baker, 2015), 85.
6. John Piper, *The Purifying Power of Living by Faith in Future Grace* (Sisters, OR: Multnomah, 1995), 132–134.
7. Slaughter, *Unfinished Business*, 158.
8. Ibid., 167–68.

Chapter 8: Our Work Is Taking Us Somewhere

1. Anne-Marie Slaughter, *Unfinished Business: Women, Men, Work, Family* (New York: Random House, 2015), 84.

2. Noel Piper, *Faithful Women and Their Extraordinary God* (Wheaton, IL: Crossway, 2005), 22–27.

3. Rachel Jankovic, *Fit to Burst: Abundance, Mayhem, and the Joys of Motherhood* (Moscow, ID: Canon Press, 2013), 25.

4. Michael Horton, *Ordinary: Sustainable Faith in a Radical, Restless World* (Grand Rapids, MI: Zondervan, 2014), 142.

5. Tom Nelson, *Work Matters: Connecting Sunday Worship to Monday Work* (Wheaton, IL: Crossway, 2011), 70–71.

6. Jennifer Senior, *All Joy and No Fun: The Paradox of Modern Parenting* (New York: Ecco, 2014), 259.

Suggested Readings

Dawn, Marva. *Keeping the Sabbath Wholly: Ceasing, Resting, Embracing, Feasting.* Grand Rapids, MI: Eerdmans, 1989.

DeYoung, Kevin. *Crazy Busy: A (Mercifully) Short Book about a (Really) Big Problem.* Wheaton, IL: Crossway, 2013.

Horton, Michael. *Ordinary: Sustainable Faith in a Radical, Restless World.* Grand Rapids, MI: Zondervan, 2014.

Jankovic, Rachel. *Fit to Burst: Abundance, Mayhem, and the Joys of Motherhood.* Moscow, ID: Canon Press, 2013.

Keller, Tim, with Katherine Leary Alsdorf. *Every Good Endeavor: Connecting Your Work to God's Work.* New York: Dutton, 2012.

McCulley, Carolyn, and Nora Shank. *The Measure of Success: Uncovering the Biblical Perspective on Women, Work, and the Home.* Nashville: B&H, 2014.

Nelson, Tom. *Work Matters: Connecting Sunday Worship to Monday Work.* Wheaton, IL: Crossway, 2011.

Norris, Kathleen. *The Quotidian Mysteries: Laundry, Liturgy, and "Women's Work."* Mahwah, NJ: Paulist Press, 1998.

Packer, J. I. *Weakness Is the Way: Life with Christ Our Strength.* Wheaton, IL: Crossway, 2013.

Peterson, Eugene. *A Long Obedience in the Same Direction: Discipleship in an Instant Society.* Downers Grove, IL: InterVarsity Press, 2000.

Piper, John. *The Purifying Power of Living by Faith in Future Grace*. Sisters, OR: Multnomah, 1995.

Piper, Noel. *Faithful Women and Their Extraordinary God*. Wheaton, IL: Crossway, 2005.

Schaeffer, Edith. *The Hidden Art of Homemaking: Creative Ideas for Enriching Everyday Life*. London: Tyndale, 1971.

Senior, Jennifer. *All Joy and No Fun: The Paradox of Modern Parenting*. New York: Ecco, 2014.

Slaughter, Anne-Marie. *Unfinished Business: Women, Men, Work, Family*. New York: Random House, 2015.

Stone, Rachel Marie. *Eat with Joy: Redeeming God's Gift of Food*. Downers Grove, IL: InterVarsity Press, 2013.

Veith, Gene Edward. *God at Work: Your Christian Vocation in All of Life*. Wheaton, IL: Crossway, 2002.

Wierenga, Emily. *Making It Home: Finding My Way to Peace, Identity, and Purpose*. Grand Rapids, MI: Baker, 2015.

Wingren, Gustaf. *Luther on Vocation*. Eugene, OR: Wipf and Stock, 1957.

General Index

Scripture Index

Also Available from Courtney Reissig

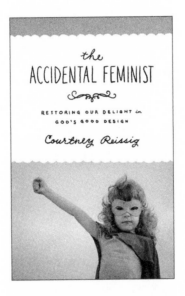

Combining personal narrative, practical examples, and biblical teaching, this book pushes back against both feminism and stereotypes related to gender roles in an effort to help Christians discover joy and purpose in God's good design for women.

For more information, visit crossway.org.